Quilting
the new classics

20 INSPIRED QUILT PROJECTS
TRADITIONAL TO MODERN DESIGNS

MICHELE MUSKA

sixth&springbooks
NEW YORK

sixth&springbooks

161 Avenue of the Americas, New York, NY 10013
sixthandspringbooks.com

Editorial Director	JOY AQUILINO
Managing Editor	KRISTINA MCGOWAN
Developmental Editor	LISA SILVERMAN
Editor	JENNIFER SPIELVOGEL
Art Director	DIANE LAMPHRON
Book Design	CHRISTINA JARUMAY FOX
Illustrations	JOHN BAUMGARTEL
Photography	JACK DEUTSCH STUDIO
Editorial Assistant	JOHANNA LEVY
Proofreader	DARYL BROWER
Vice President	TRISHA MALCOLM
Publisher	CAROLINE KILMER
Production Manager	DAVID JOINNIDES
President	ART JOINNIDES
Chairman	JAY STEIN

Library of Congress Cataloging-in-Publication Data

Muska, Michele.

Quilting the new classics : 20 inspired quilt projects:
traditional to modern designs / Michele Muska;
foreword by Meg Cox; foreword by Janneken Smucker.

    pages cm

ISBN: 978-1-93-6096-80-0

1. Quilting–United States–Patterns.
2. Patchwork–United States–Patterns. I. Title.

TT835.M93 2014

746.46--dc23

                    2014008560

Manufactured in China

1 3 5 7 9 10 8 6 4 2

First Edition

 # DEDICATION

Dedicated to Nena and Papa (in spirit) for their ever-present
love and support in all my creative adventures.

Thank you to my husband Dan for his constant support
and the bottomless cup of tea he always provides to keep me going.
To my boys Devon and Logan for their belief in me as an Artist.
And for the continued love and support I receive
from all my sweet nieces, nephews, family and friends,
and especially from my "girls," Kathy, Karen, and Tara.

 # ACKNOWLEDGEMENTS

Thanks to my friend Scott for bringing me into this industry. Over the past ten years, I have met so many amazing people and have experienced so many new things, I can hardly believe it. And thank you to Jan and Brooke for continuing to inspire me.

My sincerest thank you to my editor Joy Aquilino for her belief in my vision and her trust in my abilities, as well as everyone at Sixth & Spring Books. To my dear friends who kept me grounded in reality during this process: I thank Victoria, Susan, Jo, Darlene, Haley, Drew, Leslie, Allie and "my goddesses," Meg and Janneken, for your kind and wonderful words. Leslie Tucker Jennison, Judy Novella, and Teresa Coates, for your contribution. Amy Milne, Executive Director of The Quilt Alliance;

Pam Weeks, Curator NEQM and Marsha MacDowell of MSU Museum for working with me to secure images. A very special thank you goes to Nancy Bavor, Curator of Collections at the San Jose Museum of Quilts and Textiles. Without Nancy's generosity, I would not have been able to secure enough images to do this book justice! Roderick Kiracofe, thank you for your kindness and support. And to Barbara Parsons Cartier who was an incredible asset and tech editor... so happy we found each other again!

And lastly, but most importantly, thank you to all the artists that agreed to come on this journey with me. I love you all and the work you do. You are an inspiration to me and to the quilt and fiber world we live and work in.

Michele Muska, author and Quilt Alliance board member, will donate a portion of the proceeds of this book to Michigan State University Museum for the following, in the hopes that it will benefit The Quilt Alliance in their mission to preserve the culture and history of quilting:

The Quilt Index is a joint project of the Quilt Alliance; MATRIX: The Center for Humane Arts, Letters and Social Sciences Online at Michigan State University; and the Michigan State University Museum.

Michigan State University Museum has made a partial donation of images for this publication to further promote the documentation of quilts and quiltmakers for the future.

FOREWORD

BY JANNEKEN SMUCKER

We use the metaphor of the quilt to describe many things—any entity made up of composite parts that make a pleasing whole, or sometimes a chaotic whole (as in the case of the Crazy Quilt). We employ this turn of phrase because it makes sense, and we love to think about creatively combining individual bits and pieces to form something greater than the individual parts.

That metaphor—as overused as it sometimes feels—can be applied to the history of the quilt itself. An individual quilt can certainly be interesting, comforting, aesthetically beautiful, and associated with memories and myths. But a single quilt does not exist in a vacuum. Every quilt is tied to past quilts and past traditions, to other forms of visual culture, to its maker's ancestors, to its future use, and to all the stories we collectively tell ourselves about quilts.

In this book, Michele Muska and the contributing quiltmakers help us make those connections clearer. We can see a single quilt, existing as a beautiful individual object with a distinct story of craftsmanship, discovery, wear and tear, preservation, innovation, and adaptation. And we also see how that same quilt—or quilts in that pattern collectively—unites within a larger story of making usable and beautiful objects from cloth.

For example, Victoria Findlay Wolfe's imaginative adaptation of the Double Wedding Ring—a favorite 1930s pattern that has endured the decades—is now part of the long story this pattern tells, united by a design rife with symbolism, which also serves as a perfect canvas for playing with foreground and background and integrating diverse scraps of fabric. Each of the over 1,000 Double Wedding Ring quilts documented in the Quilt Index (a joint project of the Quilt Alliance, MATRIX: The Center for Humane Arts, Letters and Social Sciences Online, and Michigan State University Museum) share a piece of history with Victoria's modern adaptation. Every quiltmaker and every quilt is part of this ongoing conversation of adapting, innovating, and contributing to a larger, more beautiful whole.

■ Janneken Smucker is an assistant professor of history at West Chester University and the author of *Amish Quilts: Crafting and American Icon* (Johns Hopkins University Press, 2013).

FOREWORD

BY MEG COX

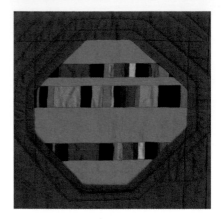

The Modern Quilt movement began in 2009, when a small group of quilters in Los Angeles who had been sharing their quilts on blogs decided they wanted to meet fellow quilters in person.

Though technology brought them together, it was traditional patterns they craved in the form of geometric shapes like hexagons and simple squares. But they didn't want to slavishly copy old block patterns like Log Cabins and Grandmother's Flower Gardens, executing them in fussy reproduction fabrics. They chose to reinvent the traditional designs in minimalist styles, usually with solid colors and often with white or gray backgrounds.

These moderns were a practical lot. They wanted to use all the tools of their time, including the latest sewing machines, and they wanted to make quilts for their loved ones' beds, not the walls.

Nobody could have predicted that the Modern movement would sweep the country so quickly;

within four years there were 180 chapters of the Modern Quilt Guild, with more than 40 of them overseas. Every fabric company and quilt shop began featuring more solid color fabrics and modern print patterns. Major quilt show producers like the American Quilter's Society began adding a modern category to their shows.

To be sure, the movement and the guild are not synonymous. There are thousands upon thousands of quilters who may never join a chapter of the Modern Quilt Guild, but still want to experiment with the modern aesthetic. These are quilters who love to explore different styles and techniques, and stay on top of the trends. They see these bright, perky new designs, and want to try their own hand at a wonky, freehand Log Cabin or stripped down Hexie quilt.

What accounts for such popularity? Curiously, the Modern movement has attracted both a younger demographic, especially young mothers in their 20s and 30s who were already part of the DIY scene, as well as older women, many who were already quilting. But the savvy founders of Modern Quilt Guild presented themselves as rebels, rule-breakers, and free spirits. Having a good time seems part of the mandate for these new guilds which have attracted established quilters, who felt rule-bound

guilds were getting ossified. This message that quiltmaking should be playful and joyful is a very contagious one.

Michele Muska is a crafter and quiltmaker always on top of the trends and personally full of joy. She is also someone who cherishes the original quilt patterns that have been adapted by the moderns, so she has compiled the perfect pairing between traditional and modern approaches. She offers quilters of all skill levels a range of fun and inspiring projects, while cherishing and explaining the roots of traditional quilting that shine through in the best modern quilts. While some quiltmakers try to foment divisions, even antagonism between the traditional and modern quilters, Michele Muska shows us how beautifully the different styles feed off one another.

The truly miraculous thing about quilting is how it continues to change, staying vital, even thrilling, as the centuries tick past. At the heart of the craft is the legacy of these established and endlessly adaptable patterns, an alphabet that keeps allowing for the creation of brand new words.

■ Meg Cox is president of the Quilt Alliance and author of the bestseller *The Quilter's Catalog: A Comprehensive Resource Guide* (Workman Publishing).

Contents

PREFACE

CLOTH HAS PROTECTED US FROM THE ELEMENTS FOR THOUSANDS OF YEARS AND HAS MADE MEN RICH.

It feeds our souls when transformed or woven into pieces of art, spun with gold and precious fibers, or simply woven into basic broadcloth. For me, any piece of cloth, whether simple or complex, is art. Its hand and texture can elicit a feeling and conjure up a specific memory. For most quilters, collecting fabric is in our makeup; we may not know how we will use it, but we do know we need it. And need is a powerful drive, especially when we create our art with fabric.

"Our stash" is what we call our fabric collection and it brings us comfort and sometimes a sense of confidence. Yards and even scraps of beautiful fabrics fill an empty spot in us late at night or during a snowstorm when we have the urge to create and sew. Our stash is always waiting for us like a dear sweet friend, providing the inspiration and materials to create quilts. Quilts keep us warm and content, celebrate new beginnings, and help us through difficult times.

Many of us have a quilt or a memory of one that is personally meaningful: Mine is a scrappy Nine Patch with half-square triangles in the corners. I made that quilt when I was about 10 years old with a bit of guidance from my mother and my 4-H leader. I made the blocks by randomly pulling fabric from my mom's stash, which included fabric from the dresses and hats she had made for us. I wonder how this Nine Patch would be categorized today. Would it be traditional or modern? I pieced the blocks together traditionally, but the juxtaposition of cotton solids and dress prints, with different widths of bright mustard color sashing made it somewhat unsettling. The sashing widths were dictated a bit by choice and a bit by the limitations of the fabric scraps. Once I finished the top, I asked my mom for an old sheet for the backing and pulled the thin flannel sheet right off my own bed for the filling. I used embroidery floss to tie the three layers together and finished my first quilt.

That Nine Patch quilt lay at the end of my bed for years and went off to college with me along with my life-size poster of Jimmy Hendrix. When I moved to Boston and got married, the quilt came with me and was thrown into the trunk of our car for picnics and beach outings. Somewhat worn, that twin-size patchwork quilt traveled to Connecticut when we moved our little family there. I still can picture the boys sitting on that quilt in the backyard of our new home.

As I look back, my first quilt is symbolic of the way I continue to work as an artist. The quilt was not planned or sketched out ahead of time and my work continues to follow this process-driven habit today. One act or decision often takes me in an entirely different direction than I initially anticipated. I wonder now what made me chose that particular Nine Patch pattern. Obviously, I took liberties with quilting patterns from the start.

If my quilt had been handed down through the generations, how much of that story would travel with the quilt? My Great Aunt Sadie's Crazy Quilt (page 26) came to me from my mom through her sister, Myrna. We don't have much personal history of the quilt except we believe it was the only quilt she ever made. Are the stories that are handed down from generation to generation about family heirlooms accurate? Sometimes when an expert authenticates a quilt, it becomes apparent that some stories are embellished or just remembered incorrectly. Today there are clues in every quilt that can direct us to its origins: The fabric print date or the type of filler that was used can help date a quilt.

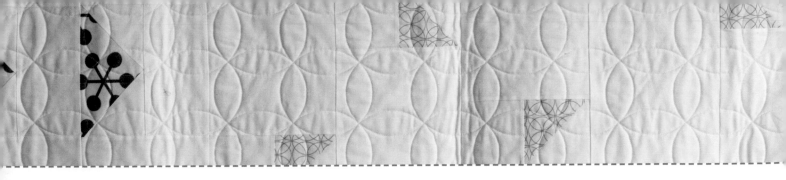

Quilts are woven into our culture so seamlessly we often forget when, how, from what, and why they were created. It is the mission of the Quilt Alliance, founded in 1993, to document and preserve quilts and share their stories and the history of the quiltmaker for future generations. Being on the board of the Quilt Alliance has made me committed to this mission. As these treasures become part of museum collections, family heirlooms, or grace our walls and beds, there is one thing I am so certain about: We always crave to know more about the quiltmaker when we stand before or lay beneath the quilt.

When I see a quilt anywhere, especially at a flea market or a museum where the maker is anonymous, a feeling of emptiness comes over me. I want to know who spent those many hours piecing the cloth together. Labeling the quilts you make is important for your own knowledge, for historical purposes, and equally important for the curious. Without a doubt, take the time to document its origin and record as many stories as you care to share.

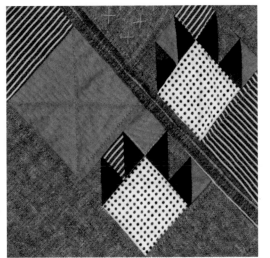

The quilts featured in this book are as artistically eclectic as I am. I personally invited quilt designers whose work I admire and who I knew would share their personal perspective, to design a quilt for this book. These designers understand the concept of embracing traditional and modern quilts together.

There are ten traditional quilt patterns represented in this book, each with its own chapter. Each chapter features photographs and a brief history of an heirloom or museum-quality quilt, along with complete how-to instructions for you to make both a contemporary/traditional quilt and a modern quilt interpretation of each pattern. Each designer chose a specific quilt pattern without ever seeing the inspirational photo or reading the historical information (with the exception of the Crazy Quilters) and had the freedom to create their own, unique adaptation of the pattern. You may draw your own conclusions to any similarities or influence!

Most of my basic historical knowledge came from looking at and discussing quilts with my family and quilting friends. Reference books either validated my basic ideas or gave me additional insight into the historical background of the quilts and patterns. It was Barbara Brackman's *Encyclopedia of Pieced Quilt Patterns* that helped me make the regional connections that quilt patterns have throughout the United States.

There was a buzz on the Quiltcon 2013 show floor about the liberties that some of the quilters had taken with construction, design, content and color. The debate was refreshing and seemed to awaken an excitement in many quiltmakers. I don't think I will ever forget the words of Luella Doss when I came across her viewing the quilts, "They are all just fabric sandwiches, right? And we all love sandwiches, don't we?" And yes, I may not fall in love with every quilt I see, but I appreciate the time, work, care and love that it took to create it.

– Michele Muska

Barbara Brackman, *Encyclopedia of Pieced Quilt Patterns.* Paducah, KY: Americans Quilter's society, 1993.

The Quilts

TRADITIONAL
MEETS MODERN

Double Wedding Ring

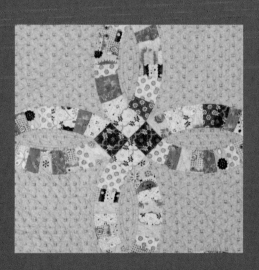

Double Wedding Ring
Collection of Roderick Kiracofe;
Maker: unknown;
found in Kansas City, Missouri;
Ca. 1940-1960; 84" x 76";
Photo by Sharon Risedorph

Double Wedding Ring
Collection of Roderick
Kiracofe; Maker: unknown;
purchased in Fayette,
Alabama; Ca. 1940 to 1960;
Cotton, hand-pieced and
quilted, yellow muslin backing
same as the front, brought
around to the front;
Photo by Sharon Risedorph.

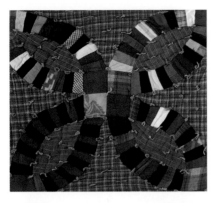

DOUBLE WEDDING RING INSPIRATION

The interconnected blocks or circles of Double Wedding Ring quilts symbolize love, something that is or should be steadfast. Unbreakable! It is probably one of the most recognizable quilt blocks among non-quilters today. The Double Wedding Ring gained popularity in the 1930s among the broader quilting public. Small print fabrics and pastel colors were top choices, but those who had suffered most during the Depression gravitated toward a bolder palette. Earlier versions of this pattern, pre-20th century, were called Rainbow, Around the World, Endless Chain, King Tut and Friendship Knot.*

This intricate pattern, with its many curves, was rarely attempted by beginning quilters. However, today's acrylic templates and die cutters make cutting exact pattern pieces easy, and have enabled a whole new group of quilters to be very successful. The variations on this interlocking ringed pattern are many. Modern quilters, in particular, love to explore and integrate negative space into their designs. The quilting is often highlighted in the center space to create several focal points or a space to rest the eyes. It's exciting that a pattern that symbolizes love is having its own love affair with modern and contemporary quilters today. And perhaps only a modern quilter has the strength to break the rings and push the design elements in an entirely new direction.

Shelly Pagliai and Victoria Findlay Wolfe's Double Wedding Ring quilts are similarly constructed. Both use modern acrylic templates, yet with very different results. The fabric choices and placements of each designer dictate the overall aesthetic of the finished quilts.

*Pg. 136, *Minnesota Quilts, Creating a Connection With Our Past;* Voyager Press 2005.

TRADITIONAL
DOUBLE WEDDING RING

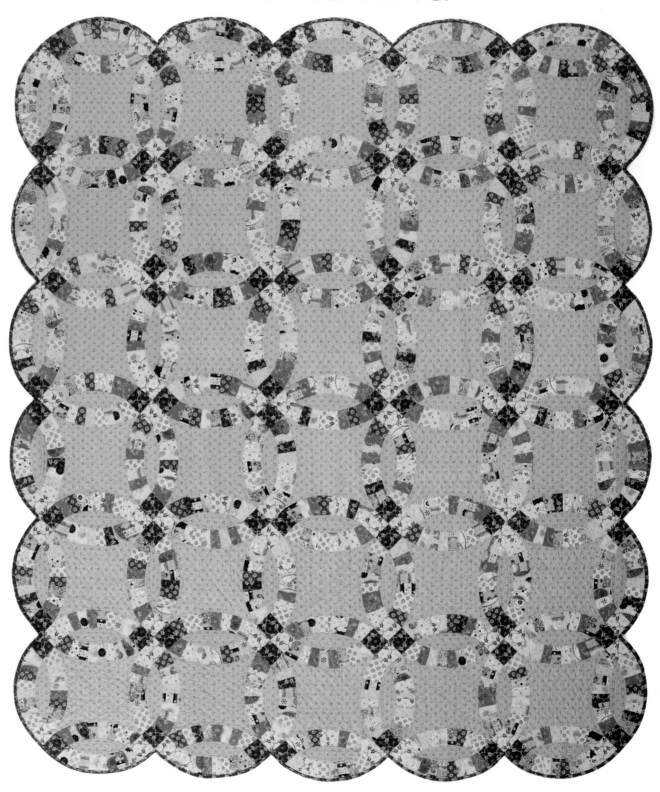

A Graceful Wedding

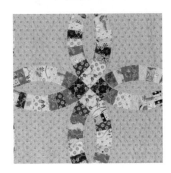

INSPIRATION

I always envision the Double Wedding Ring Quilt in soft colors with a scrappy, yet controlled look. For my version of this traditional and well-loved quilt, I chose fabrics from one collection. I mixed them up to create the scrappy look I was after, yet kept the certain soft palette I desired. I chose traditional motifs for the quilting, and put feathers in the large open areas, to maintain the quilt's soft and elegant, old-fashioned feel.

DESIGNED, PIECED AND QUILTED BY SHELLY PAGLIAI

FINISHED DIMENSIONS Approximately 70" wide x 83" long

FABRIC

Use a great variety of prints to achieve the best scrappy look. I used a fat quarter bundle of 21 fat quarters from the Twig & Grace Collection by Sue Daley Designs for Riley Blake Designs. Yardages are based on 44"/45"-wide fabrics.

Various prints: 5¼ yards total for the rings

Pink print: 4 yards for background

Brown print: 1⅝ yards for connecting squares and bias binding

Cream print: ⅝ yard for connecting squares

Backing fabric: 6 yards of 44/45"-wide OR 2½ yards of 108"-wide

Batting: 2¼ yards of 93"-wide batting

SUPPLIES

- General Sewing Supplies (page 150)
- EZ Quilting Tools Simpli-EZ Double Wedding Ring #8829419A by Darlene Zimmerman or template on page 142

SHELLY PAGLIAI

Shelly credits her grandmother, Mildred, for starting her down the road of quilting obsession. Mildred enrolled her in 4-H sewing classes at the age of eight. One thing led to another, and in 1999, Prairie Moon Quilts (www.prairiemoonquilts.com) was born. From her home studio, Shelly sells her original quilt patterns and kits, and does professional machine quilting for other quilters. When she's not teaching classes, selling her designs, operating the longarm, running her charity "Necktie Social," or creating her own award-winning, nationally exhibited quilts, Shelly can be found spending time with her favorite cowboy and all of their many animals on their Missouri ranch.

CUTTING THE FABRIC

1. RINGS

Use the wedge templates provided with the Simpli-Ez Double Wedding Ring tool or the template on page 139.

From the various ring fabrics (or scraps):

- Use the wedge template A to cut 852 pieces
- Use the wedge template B to cut 142 pieces
- Use the wedge template B **reversed** to cut 142 pieces

2. CONNECTING SQUARES

Use the Simpli-Ez Double Wedding Ring tool to cut the squares or the template on page 139.

- Brown fabric—cut 71 squares
- Cream fabric—cut 71 squares

3. SMALL MELONS

Use the Simpli-Ez Double Wedding Ring tool or the template on page 139 to cut the small melons.

- Pink fabric—cut 71 melons

4. BACKGROUND

Use the Simpli-Ez Double Wedding Ring tool to cut the curved edges.

- Pink fabric—30 squares, each 10¼" x 10¼"

SEWING INSTRUCTIONS

All seams are sewn right sides together using a ¼" seam allowance unless otherwise indicated.

Assemble the Rings

1. Sew together six A-wedge pieces to make an arc, mixing up your fabrics to create a scrappy look.

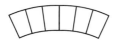

2. Stitch a B-wedge piece to the right end of the arc, and a B-wedge reversed piece to the left end of the arc. Press all seams to one side.

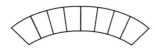

3. Repeat to create a second arc. To this second arc, add a brown connecting square to one end, and a cream connecting square to the opposite end. Press seams toward the squares.

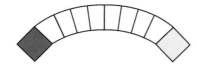

4. With the arc on top, pin centers together and sew a background melon to the first arc as shown. Press the seam toward the background melon.

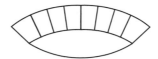

5. Add the second arc to this unit, matching centers and the connecting squares on the ends of the first arc. Press the seam toward the melon.

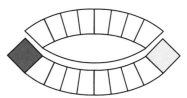

6. You now have one "melon" completed. Repeat steps 1–5 until you have made 71 melons.

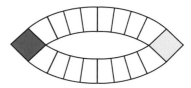

ASSEMBLING THE QUILT TOP

1. Now you're ready to set the quilt together. It may help to lay the entire quilt out on a design wall to make sure you have an even distribution of color, and that your connecting squares are all in the correct positions. Pay special attention to the following diagrams to make sure that you have the melons turned correctly so that the connecting squares make the proper design in the finished quilt.

2. Sew the melons to the center background pieces, matching centers, and making sure the connecting squares line up. Press seams toward the center background pieces. Make a total of 30 units as shown below, making sure the position of the brown and cream squares match the diagrams. You will have 11 melons left; save them for a later step.

- Make 15 units like this, using one background piece and two melons. Note the position of the brown and cream connecting squares.

- Make 15 units like this, using one background piece and two melons. Note the position of the brown and cream connecting squares.

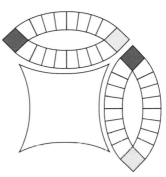 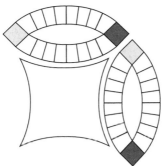

3. Sew these units together as shown, into rows of five units, alternating the units and making sure you have them turned correctly. (You should always be sewing a cream connecting square to a brown connecting square where they meet up.)

4. Make six rows. Sew the rows together, matching up the connecting squares carefully.

5. Use the remaining 11 melons to fill in the gaps across the top and bottom and down the right side of the quilt.

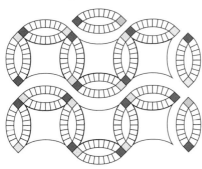

FINISHING THE QUILT

1. If using 44"/45"-wide fabric for the back, cut and piece the backing fabric to create a backing that is at least 4" to 6" larger than the quilt-top measurements.

2. Prepare the quilt sandwich and machine- or hand-quilt as desired (see page 154). Trim the edges.

3. Make bias binding from the brown print fabric (see page 155).

4. Sew binding to the front side of quilt with right sides together, folding binding to miter at each outer point (see page 155). Turn the binding and slipstitch the binding to the back side.

MODERN
DOUBLE WEDDING RING

Modern Love

INSPIRATION

When I was contemplating which modern fabric to use for this traditional quilt pattern, I realized that a chevron print really fit the bill nicely! It is a graphic design that has been used over and over, in both modern and traditional quilts. And I love that it crosses all the lines in quilt making. Adding in the Cherrywood Hand Dyed Fabrics (see resources on page 158) really made everything pop. My success was marked when my daughter came into my studio and said, "Wow! I love it! It's so modern!"

DESIGNED, PIECED, AND QUILTED BY VICTORIA FINDLAY WOLFE

FINISHED DIMENSIONS Approximately 43" wide x 43" long

FABRIC

Yardages are based on 44"/45"-wide fabric.

Bright green solid:
1 yard for rings

Tan solid:
⅛ yard for center ring

Chevron print:
⅔ yard for background

Gray solid: ½ yard or a fat quarter for center background

White faux bois print:
⅓ yard for small melons

White with mini dots:
¼ yard for connecting squares

Dark purple solid: 1⅓ yards for connecting squares, small melons, and corners (includes 1 yard for bias binding)

Backing: 2 yards

Batting: Crib size

SUPPLIES

- General Sewing Supplies (page 150)
- EZ Quilting Tools Simpli-EZ Double Wedding Ring #8829419A by Darlene Zimmerman or template on page 139
- EZ Quilting Tools Simpli-EZ Double Wedding Ring Single Arc tool #882157001A by Darlene Zimmerman or template on page 139

■ **VICTORIA FINDLAY WOLFE**

Victoria is a New York City-based fabric designer and award-winning quilter. This multi-talented quilter won "Best in Show" at QuiltCon 2013, and is the author of *15 Minutes of Play* (C&T Publishing). Victoria is also the founder of NYC MOD quilters, board member of the Quilt Alliance and International Quilt Association, and runs several community drives with BumbleBeansBASICS. Born and raised on a farm in Minnesota, Victoria credits her grandmother's double-knit crazy quilts—which kept her warm growing up—for influencing her love of quilting. Her biggest supporters are her husband and daughter. You can learn more about Victoria at www.bumblebeansbasics.com.

CUTTING THE FABRIC

1. RINGS

Use the Simpli-Ez Double Wedding Ring Single Arc tool or the arc template on page 139 to cut the arcs.

- Bright green solid—cut 44 arcs
- Tan solid—cut four arcs

2. BACKGROUND

Use the Simpli-Ez Double Wedding Ring Tool or the template on page 140 to cut the curved edges.

- Chevron print—cut eight squares each 10¼" x 10¼"
- Gray solid—cut one square 10¼" x 10¼"

3. SMALL MELONS

Use the Simpli-Ez Double Wedding Ring tool or the template on page 140 to cut the melons.

- White faux bois print— cut 16 melons
- Dark purple solid— cut eight melons

4. CONNECTING SQUARES

Use the Simpli-Ez Double Wedding Ring tool or the template on page 140 to cut the connecting squares.

- White with mini dots print— cut 32 squares
- Dark purple solid—cut 24 squares

5. POINTED CORNERS

Use Template A, provided on page 139, to cut the pointed corners.

- Dark purple solid—cut four pointed corners

SEWING INSTRUCTIONS

All seams are sewn right sides together using a ¼" seam allowance unless otherwise indicated.

Arrange all pieces as shown on a design wall or other flat surface. Follow the photo for fabric placement.

Constructing the Melons

1. Fold one arc in half and lightly finger-press to find the center of the inside curve. Unfold. Do the same for the small melon. With the arc on top and right sides together, pin centers together and sew the curved seam.

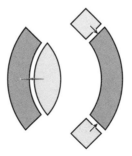

To the opposite arc, sew the connecting squares to each end.

2. Sew these two units together, pinning centers and matching up the connecting squares to the ends of the first arc. You now have one "melon" completed.

3. Repeat steps 1–2 until you have constructed all 24 melons. You will have eight dark purple connecting squares and the four pointed corners left over to attach later.

ASSEMBLING THE QUILT

Pay special attention to the diagrams to make sure that you have the pieces turned correctly so they create the proper design in the finished quilt.

1. In vertical rows, sew the horizontal melons to the center background pieces, matching centers.

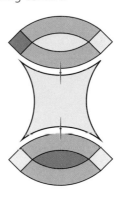

2. Sew the vertical melons to the center background pieces, on alternating sides as shown, matching up the connecting squares.

3. Sew the rows together, matching up the connecting squares carefully. Use the remaining pieces to fill in the sides.

FINISHING THE QUILT

1. Prepare the quilt sandwich and machine- or hand-quilt as desired (see page 154). Trim the edges.

2. Make bias binding from the solid purple fabric (see page 155).

3. Sew the binding to the front side of quilt with right sides together, folding the binding to miter at each outer point. At each inner point, clip the quilt a scant ¼" through all layers. Gently stretch the quilt at these points to sew the binding on straight (no folds on inner corners).

clip quilt, scant ¼"

4. Turn the binding and hand-sew the binding to the back side.

5. Don't forget to add a label to your new heirloom!

Crazy Quilt

Wool Strip Crazy Quilt
Gift to the San Jose Museum of Quilts
and Textiles from Roderick Kiracofe;
Photo by Sharon Risedorph

Crazy Quilt
Collection of Joyce Muska; Maker: Sadie (Sarah) Lovely
Mullen 1878–1973; Ca. 1930; 53" x 70"; Corinna, ME;
Rayon prints and solid colored dress fabrics, mitered corners,
embroidery, batting evident and tied

Three Owls Crazy Quilt
Maker: Elizabeth Parkhurst Williams
and Mrs. Edward C. (Mae) Parkhurst;
Ca. 1884-1890; Silk, satin, historic ribbons,
silk yarns; embroidered border and central
panel; San Jose Museum of Quilts and Textiles

Crazy Quilt "For Uncle Hal, with Love"
Maker: Allie Aller;
Ca. 2008; 40" x 40"

CRAZY QUILT INSPIRATION

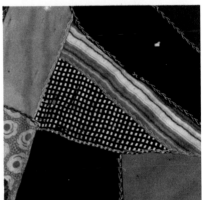

■ The quilt on the top right of the facing page was authenticated at an Ashville, North Carolina quilt turning by Merikay Waldvogel, who was more excited by the back of the quilt than the front. The back is constructed of large square blocks of oversized rayon dress prints and a white solid.

My great aunt Sadie made this Crazy Quilt during the 1930s. As far as we know, it is the only quilt she ever made. It came to my mother, Joyce Lovely Muska, through her sister from Fort Fairfield, Maine in the 1980s. The quilt is somewhat typical of the simpler crazy quilt method you might find in rural New England.

Crazy quilts were some of the first quilts that were made for purely decorative purposes in the latter half of the 19th and early 20th centuries. Women were excited to show off their needlework skills and often purchased dress and specialty fabrics to finish their pieces. Quilters with limited time, whom could not produce a full-size quilt, could make smaller decorative pieces. Initially, Crazy Quilts were met with some resistance by traditional quilters, but became widely accepted and sold for considerable amounts of money by the early 1900s. They lost some popularity during the 20s.

"People come to crazy quilting from so many different back-grounds. Traditional makers of quilts 'go crazy' of course, but many crazy quilters start out in embroidery, cross-stitching, painting, tatting, or even mixed media. And truly, any needlework or fiber technique can be incorporated into a Crazy Quilt. That's what keeps it so fresh with possibilities." *

■ So, it seems that Crazy Quilts are being celebrated again! Val Bothell's sweet Crazy Quilt epitomizes the true art of crazy quilting, the perfection of the needlework, and the asymmetrical placement of the fabrics. Allie Aller has set her design on point and allows the negative space to make the center motifs pop in a fresh, modern approach. Her clever placement of the trim gives the quilt even more complexity without the added needlework.

Allie Aller's Crazy Quilting; C & T Publishing Inc., pg 7

TRADITIONAL
CRAZY QUILT

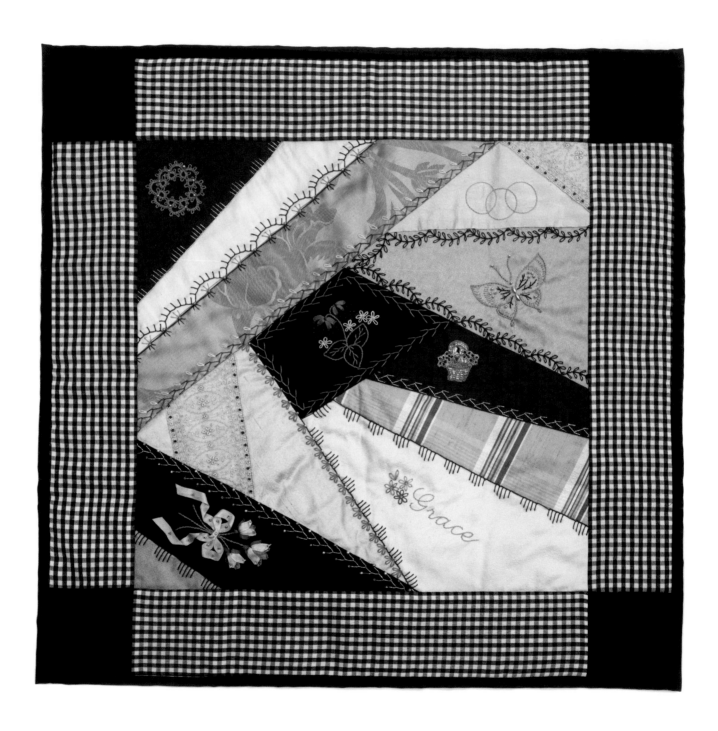

Tamar Came to Visit

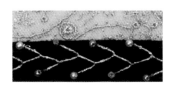

INSPIRATION

Crazy quilting has been my passion for the last 16 years. One of my favorite Crazy Quilts is owned by the Metropolitan Museum of Art in New York City and was made by Tamar Horton Harris North in 1877 in memory of her deceased daughter Grace. I have always wanted to use this Crazy Quilt as inspiration to make my own version of what Tamar did so well over 130 years ago.

First, I foundation pieced a 16½" block with a basic flip-and-sew method using Tamar's color choices as inspiration. Then I embroidered and embellished the block to my heart's content. I added a 3½" black-and-white checked border with 3½" black square insets at each corner. The finished piece was then layered like a sandwich with the backing, batting, and completed blocked top. I tied the layers together with black pearl cotton to keep them secure and added a black fabric binding.

DESIGNED, PIECED AND QUILTED BY VALERIE BOTHELL

FINISHED DIMENSIONS Approximately 23½" square

FABRIC

Please feel free to make different color choices for your project to make it personal to you. Yardages are based on 44"/45"-wide fabric.

Brocade: red and blue
⅓ yard of each

Silk dupioni: pink, grey, ivory, black-and-blue plaid
⅓ yard of each

Black-and-white checked fabric: ½ yard

Muslin: 1 yard

Black satin for backing and binding: 1 yard

Batting: American Spirit Superior Blend by Fairfield, 25" square

SUPPLIES

- General Sewing Supplies (page 150)
- Template (block diagram on page 141)
- Neutral colored thread for foundation piecing
- Embroidery threads in colors that coordinate with your fabric choices. (Pearl cotton, silk buttonhole twist and Kreinik #4 Braid are my favorites.)

- #24 chenille needle for embroidery
- Scraps of lace and/or tatting for embellishment
- Optional 7mm silk ribbon in light pink, dark pink and blue (I use RiverSilks)

VALERIE BOTHELL

Valerie Bothell has been happily teaching crazy quilting from her home in Wichita, Kansas for the last 17 years and has hosted the Victorian Stitchery Retreat for the last seven years in Wichita. Traveling and teaching is very rewarding to her, and she always looks forward to every opportunity to share her love of crazy quilting. She has been married for 20 years and has four very handsome sons. You may visit her website at www.valeriebothell.com.

MODERN
CRAZY QUILT

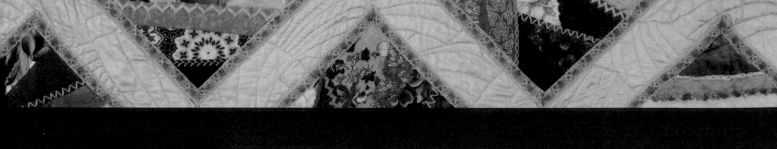

Simply Crazy

DESIGNED, PIECED, AND QUILTED BY ALLIE ALLER

FINISHED DIMENSIONS Approximately 72" wide x 72" long

INSPIRATION

I adore crazy quilting and have been searching for new ways to interpret the genre. This Crazy Quilt has an unusual construction sequence, which gives it a fresh and original look. It is a functional quilt, too, not just decorative!

Using an atypical technique, a whole cloth quilt sandwich is first machine quilted in a freeform, overall design. Then nine blocks and four border strips are crazy pieced on muslin foundations, using both a pattern and freeform flip-and-sew techniques. Blocks and border strips are then embroidered by hand and machine. The completed blocks and borders are raw-edge appliquéd onto the quilted top with their edges subsequently finished with appliquéd ribbon. Finally, additional ribbon serves to bind the quilt.

FABRIC

Kaufman Radiance, a 50/50 blend of silk and cotton, in champagne color was used for the whole cloth quilt top. The scraps chosen were bright colors with a few large-scale floral prints. Feel free to substitute your own choices to make the quilt your own. Yardages are based on 44"/45"-wide fabric.

Champagne color fabric:
4¼ yards for the whole cloth quilt top

Red solid cotton:
4¼ yards for quilt backing

Muslin: 2 yards for block and border foundations

Scraps (your color choice):
Approximately 3 yards total

1½"-wide jacquard ribbon:
6 yards for outer border edges

¾"-wide jacquard ribbon:
5 yards for inner border edges

⅝"-wide jacquard ribbon:
12 yards to surround the blocks

1½"-wide plaid rayon taffeta ribbon:
8½ yards for the binding

Batting: Queen-size Machine 60/40 Blend cotton/polyester by Fairfield

Martha Negley for Rowan Fabrics. Westminster Fi...

ALLIE ALLER

Allie Aller graduated from Cornell University with a degree in design and has been quilting ever since. Her first love is crazy quilting and she has written two books on the subject for C & T Publishing: *Allie Aller's Crazy Quilting: Modern Piecing* and *Embellishing Techniques for*

Joyful Stitching, and with Valerie Bothell, *Quilting… Just a Little Bit Crazy: A Marriage of Traditional* and *Crazy Quilting*. Allie also teaches crazy quilting for Craftsy. Her quilts have won numerous national awards and she is always looking to break new ground.

SUPPLIES

- General Sewing Supplies (page 150)
- Template (block diagram on page 141)
- 50-weight, neutral-colored thread for flip-and-sew foundation piecing
- Invisible thread for appliqué
- Several colors of 12-weight machine thread for machine embroidery

- 50-weight neutral thread for bobbin
- 50-weight red thread for bobbin
- 50-weight cream thread for top
- Several colors of 4mm, 7mm, and 12mm silk ribbon for optional ribbon embroidery (I prefer RiverSilks for its high thread count)

- 80/12 jeans or topstitching needle (Large eye for invisible thread sewing)
- 100/16 jeans or topstitching needle for machine embroidery with 12-weight thread
- Size 18 chenille needle for ribbon embroidery
- Tracing paper and drawing ruler

SEWING INSTRUCTIONS

All seams are sewn right sides together using a ½" seam allowance unless otherwise indicated.

Making the Whole Cloth Quilt Sandwich

1. Cut the 4½ yards of whole cloth quilt top fabric in half, yielding two pieces about 80" long.

2. Sew the two pieces together to make the quilt top. From that center seam, measure and mark each half to 40"-wide and trim. Your whole cloth top is 80" x 80".

3. Repeat Steps 1 and 2 for the quilt backing.

4. Trim batting to 80" x 80".

5. On a large flat surface, layer the quilt backing right side down, then the quilt batting, and finally the whole cloth quilt top right side up. Pin-baste or baste using any method of your choice. (See page 153 for basting and quilting tips.)

6. Using the cream thread on top and red thread in the bobbin, machine-quilt the entire quilt in an overall pattern of your choice, remembering that some of it will be covered on the front of the quilt, though all will show nicely on the quilt's back.

Preparing the Block and Border Diagrams and Foundations

1. Trace the block diagram, including the numbers, as given on page 141 for Valerie Bothell's traditional crazy quilt. Enlarge your drawing until it is 10" square. Make a second enlargement of the same size, only reversed. Put an "R" next to the numbers on the reversed copy. This gives you two different but related block diagrams. You will need two copies of each enlargement: one for templates and one for a reference.

2. Prepare your muslin foundations. Cut four pieces each 6" x 48" for the borders, and nine squares 10" x 10" for the blocks.

3. Using a light table or window, trace the original enlarged block diagram onto five squares of muslin; trace the reversed diagram onto the remaining four muslin squares. Use a disappearing ink fabric marker, as permanent lines can show through if light color fabrics are used. Do not mark the border strips.

4. Cut apart each remaining copy of both the original and reversed diagrams. Don't mix the pieces up! Keep the pieces in separate baggies until you need them. These are your templates.

Foundation Piecing the Blocks

1. Start with one of the original block diagram muslin squares and gather your chosen scraps for your first block.

2. Pin template piece 1 right side up onto the right side of the first fabric. Draw around the shape (a ruler will help with this). Remove the template (a good practice is to put it directly back into its baggie for future use). Now draw a second line ½" beyond the first marked line, all the way around the piece. Cut out the fabric on the outer line. The ½" extra is the seam allowance.

3. Repeat for the remaining 11 template pieces until all 12 are marked and cut out. The numbers indicate the sequence in which the pieces will be sewn onto the foundation muslin.

4. Place and pin piece 1 right side up over its marked place on the foundation muslin, also right side up.

5. Place piece 2 over piece 1, right sides together using the marked lines to help position it properly along the common edge between 1 and 2. Pin into place. Sew the seam with a ½" seam allowance. Flip piece 2 over so that it is right side up and iron it flat along the seam.

6. Repeat with pieces 3 through 12 until the entire foundation muslin is covered and all 12 pieces are sewn into place.

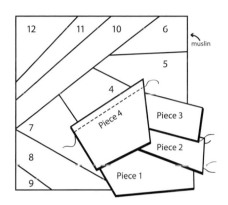

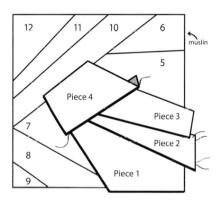

7. Sew around the perimeter of the block, ⅛" in from the edge. You will trim the block square later.

8. Repeat to make the remaining eight blocks: four more of the original diagram and four of the reversed diagram. When finished piecing, you will have five original-diagram pieced and four reverse-diagram pieced for a total of nine blocks.

Freeform Foundation Piecing the Borders (No Pattern)

Now that you have had practice flipping and sewing blocks, it is easy to make the leap to cutting out freeform shapes as you go: sewing, flipping, and pressing them open into place along the length of the border foundations. Keep the border piecing in the same scale as the blocks.

Embroidering the Blocks and Border Strips

I strove to convey the *feel* of classic crazy quilting, while being more liberated with its stitching conventions in three distinct ways:

■ Not all the seams in my quilt are covered with embroidered "seam treatments." There are just enough to suggest that charming practice, without covering all of them. But if you want to, please do!

■ I made my stitching large scale and graphic, even while using traditional crazy quilt stitches. (See page 30 of Valerie Bothell's for embroidery stitch instructions.)

■ I included some machine stitching with my handwork, employing the largest-scaled and simplest stitches my basic sewing machine had to offer: a large zigzag and a featherstitch. Using 12-weight thread and the largest settings keeps these "seam treatments" in scale with the handwork. And of course, it is much faster.

APPLIQUÉING THE BLOCKS AND BORDERS ONTO THE WHOLE CLOTH QUILT SANDWICH

Measuring and marking the center of the whole cloth quilt sandwich provides guidelines for block placement. Use a disappearing ink fabric marker, as permanent lines can show through if light fabrics are used. Once the blocks are sewn in place, the borders are added. The blocks and borders are then framed with ribbons as embellishments.

Marking the Top for Block and Border Placement

1. Measure and mark exactly 72" x 72" on your whole cloth quilt sandwich. This will be your finished, bound edge. Use the seam in the quilt top as your center. Measure and mark the width with an equal 36" on each side of the seam.

2. Find and mark the center of the length of the quilt on each side, at 36" down from the top. Draw a line across the center of the quilt.

3. Draw diagonal lines connecting the centers of each side, creating a diamond shape within the square quilt.

4. Measure and mark the center point of each diagonal line, ideally at 25". Draw two lines connecting these points, opposite each other on the diamond, making an "X" inside the diamond. Use these lines to help orient your blocks and borders.

Your quilt's marking should look like the diagram below. The border placement is included for reference.

Trimming and Appliquéing Blocks and Borders

1. Use a rotary cutter and ruler to trim each block to 9½" x 9½".

2. Trim each border strip to 5½" x 47".

3. Using the marked lines on the whole cloth quilt sandwich as a guide, place the first block on point exactly in the center of the quilt. Pin into place.

4. Sew the block onto the quilt using a straight stitch around its trimmed, raw edged perimeter. The bobbin thread should be the same as you used when quilting the whole cloth; the top thread will not show later.

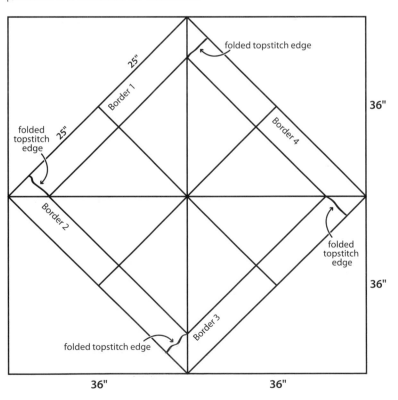

5. Pin the remaining eight blocks into place, using the marked lines for reference. Don't forget to rotate them for variation. There should be 3" between the blocks. Use a ruler! Sew the blocks to the quilt as in step 4.

6. On a large flat surface (I used the floor), position border 1 with its outer edge on the diagonal line between the top and left hand side, starting with its upper corner at the top of the diamond. The strip will not reach all the way to the corner at the left side of the diamond; that is where border 2 will start. Position border 2 along the left edge diagonal line, toward the bottom of the diamond. Border 3 starts at the bottom corner and extends along the right edge. Border 4 completes the diamond, starting at the right corner and extending to the top.

7. Pin the positioned borders into place, folding under each end that overlaps its adjacent strip at a right angle. Sew them all down as you did the blocks, topstitching along the folded end edges of each border strip.

Appliquéing Ribbons to Frame Block and Border Edges

1. Pin the ⅝"-wide ribbon all the way around the first block, starting just past a corner, centering it over the raw edge of the block. Fold and pin a miter into each corner. When you reach where you started after going all around the block, fold under the ribbon's end to cover the raw-edged beginning.

2. Use invisible thread in the top and the matching quilting thread in the bobbin. Topstitch the inner and outer edges of the ribbon frame, sewing the miters closed as you stitch.

3. Repeat steps 1 and 2 for all remaining blocks.

4. Use the ¾"-wide ribbon to frame the inner border edge, pinning and mitering the corners as with the blocks. Sew the ribbon down as in step 2.

5. Pin the 1½"-wide ribbon around the outside of the border diamond. Overlap the ends at 90 degrees at each corner, extending them beyond the marked outer perimeter of the whole cloth quilt sandwich. Topstitch the inner and outer edges as in step 2.

FINISHING AND BINDING THE QUILT WITH RIBBON

1. Sew just inside the marked perimeter line of the whole cloth quilt sandwich, to stabilize its edge. Trim the sandwich on the marked line, just beyond the stitching.

2. Iron the entire length of the plaid taffeta ribbon in half.

3. Slip the ironed plaid taffeta ribbon over the edge of the quilt sandwich so that the fold of the ribbon is snug against the edge. Pin the ribbon into place all the way around the quilt, mitering at the corners. Fold over the narrow end of the ribbon where it overlaps its raw-edged beginning, as before.

4. You can either hand-stitch first the front of the binding to the quilt sandwich and then the back with a whipstitch, or use a wide zigzag machine stitch to attach the binding in one pass. In either case, use thread that matches the binding ribbon.

Dresden Plate

Dresden Plate
Maker: Harriet Jackson
Wood Nielson; Ca. 1934;
96" x 74"; Cotton; San Jose
Museum of Quilts & Textiles

DRESDEN PLATE INSPIRATION

The Dresden pattern is extremely versatile, which is probably why it has always been such a popular design. Quilters use it as a full circle or "plate," or as a quarter circle or "fan." It is widely featured side by side as a border to frame a different feature pattern or as a fan in the corners of crazy quilts. Especially popular from the 1920s to 1950s, the wedges were often rounded and called ice cream cones or pointed to look more like a flower. Old silk ties were the perfect shape to make the Dresden wedge-shaped pieces and were a popular fabric choice. Feed sacks, which were readily available during those years, were also used; many of the vintage Dresden quilts we find today are made from them. Quilters also used the negative space between the plates to show off stitching skills, and you will often find fancy needlework stitches around the plates and wedges, as in this Harriet Nielson quilt. Harriet appliquéd whimsical bull's-eyes between the plates and then quilted graduated circles in the negative space. This Dresden pattern is also known as the Friendship Ring, Dresden Plate and Aster.*

The Dresden happens to be my personal favorite, partially because of how many ways you can configure the wedge and also because of its simplicity. My friend and fellow quilter, Darlene Zimmerman introduced me to this pattern over ten years ago and even though she tells me that there are other shapes and templates I should try, I often tell her that I am just not finished with the Dresden yet.

■ Amy Smart's sweet Dresden plate quilt is traditional in construction with a freshness that comes from her winning combination of fabric prints. Marci Warren-Elmer's deconstructed wedge takes full advantage of the simplicity of the pattern while she manipulates it in a very modern way. Both quilts are wonderful representations of the complete versatility of the Dresden pattern.

*Pg. 420, #3488.a, *Encyclopedia of Pieced Quilt Patterns*, complied by Barbara Brackman AQS

TRADITIONAL
DRESDEN PLATE

Monochromatic Dresden Plates

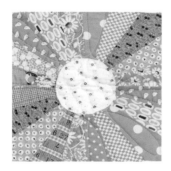

INSPIRATION

Very traditional Dresden Plate quilt blocks inspired this quilt. I wanted to use the traditional design and make it scrappy, but give it a contemporary twist by making each plate monochromatic. In the end though, the colorful, wedge border is my favorite part.

DESIGNED, PIECED, AND QUILTED BY AMY SMART

FINISHED DIMENSIONS Approximately 64" wide x 64" long

FABRIC

White print: Four–five assorted ¾ yard pieces for background

Red prints: Five–six assorted fat quarters for Dresden wedges

Yellow prints: Five–six assorted fat quarters for Dresden wedges

Blue prints: Five–six assorted fat quarters for Dresden wedges

Green prints: Five–six assorted fat quarters for Dresden wedges

Orange prints: Two–three assorted fat quarters for Dresden wedges

Blue gingham: ½ yard for sashing

Red gingham: ⅝ yard for binding

Yellow print: 4 yards for backing

Batting: Twin size

NOTE: It is very easy to cut Dresden wedges from assorted scraps as well.

SUPPLIES

- General Sewing Supplies (page 150)
- EZ Quilting Tools Easy Dresden Quilt Tool Set #882700 by Darlene Zimmerman or template on page 142

AMY SMART

Amy Smart's mother taught her how to sew, quilt, and hoard fabric. Amy worked in a local quilt shop for eight years, where she taught beginning quilting classes and where she could help new quilters fall in love with her hobby. In 2008, she discovered the online quilting community and started writing her own blog, *Diary of a Quilter* (www.diaryofaquilter.com), to document her creations and teach a whole new audience how to quilt through online tutorials. Her favorite quilts are busy, scrappy ones—whether they're old pioneer quilts, depression-era feed sack quilts, or modern designs. Amy lives in Utah with her husband and four children where they love to hike and explore the National Parks, and laugh at silly YouTube videos.

CUTTING THE FABRIC

To cut multiple Dresden wedges, cut a 6"-wide strip of fabric. Use wedge ruler to cut a wedge from that strip, and then rotate the wedge ruler 180 degrees to cut the next wedge. Repeat.

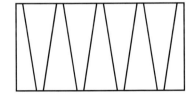

1. From the white-background print fabrics cut:

- Nine 18" x 18" squares for the Dresden plate backgrounds
- Nine 4¼" x 4¼" squares for the circle centers
- Eighty 6" Dresden wedge pieces for the borders, using the wedge ruler

2. From the assorted red, yellow, blue, and green fat quarters or scraps, use the wedge ruler to cut:

- Sixty 6" Dresden wedge pieces from each color

3. From the assorted orange fat quarters or scraps, use the wedge ruler to cut:

- Twenty-four 6" Dresden wedges

4. Cut from the blue gingham:

- 11 strips, 1¼" x width of fabric for sashing

5. Cut from the red gingham:

- Enough 2½" wide bias strips to create 275" of continuous bias binding

SEWING INSTRUCTIONS

All seams are sewn right sides together using a ¼" seam allowance unless otherwise indicated.

Constructing the Dresden Plate Blocks

1. Choose 20 monochromatic wedges for each "plate" block. Fold each wedge in half lengthwise and sew across the wide end of the wedge. Backstitch to secure and leave a thread tail at the folded end. Carefully clip the corner off the folded end.

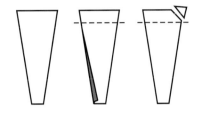

2. Press the seam open and turn the wedge right side out so the seam is hidden and there is a pointed end on the wedge. Make sure the seam is centered in the back and press the point flat. Repeat with all 20 wedges per plate. Arrange them in a circle with the points facing out.

3. Match up two wedges, right sides together, and sew down one of the long sides. Press the seam open. Sew the wedges like this into four sets of five wedges. Then sew two of the quarters together to make two halves. Match up the halves right sides together and sew the final two seams to create the full "plate" or circle of 20 wedges.

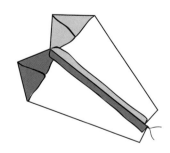

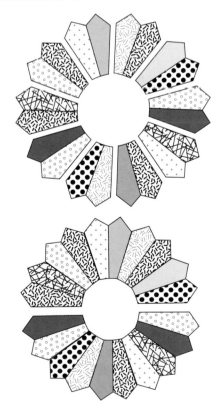

4. Appliqué the plate to one of the 18" x 18" light-background squares. To center the plate on the background square, fold the background square into four quarters and press the folds to create a crossmark in the center of the square. Use the cross as a guide for centering the Dresden plate.

5. Appliqué the block in place using preferred appliqué method.

6. To create the center circle, make a 4"-diameter circle template from plastic or cardboard. Place the template in the center of a 4½" x 4½" white background square and trim the corners to form a circle. Stitch around the edge of the fabric circle with a large running stitch and gather the edge to create a tight circle over the template. Starch lightly and press the fabric with the template still inside. Remove the template and appliqué the circle in the center of the Dresden block.

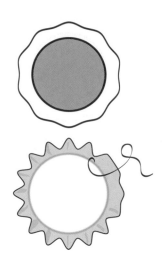

7. Repeat to make nine plates total: two each of red, yellow, blue, and green, and one orange.

ASSEMBLING THE QUILT TOP

1. Square up the Dresden plate blocks to 17" x 17".

2. Cut six strips 1¼" x 17" from three of the blue gingham strips. From the eight remaining blue gingham strips, create four 1¼" x 51½" strips and two 1¼" x 53" strips.

3. Lay out the Dresden blocks three across by three down. Lay out the six 1¼" x 17" blue gingham strips between the three blocks in each row; stitch them together. Press the seam allowances toward the sashing strips.

4. Sew the four 1¼" x 51½" blue gingham strips between the three rows and to the top and bottom of the pieced section. Press the seam allowances toward the sashing. Sew the final two 1¼" x 53" blue gingham strips to the sides of pieced unit and press the seam allowances toward the sashing.

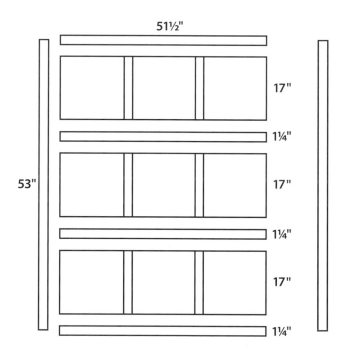

4. Make the borders. Sew 19 dark-color wedges alternating with 18 white print wedges, rotated the opposite direction. Press the seam allowances toward the dark wedges. Create three more similar units.

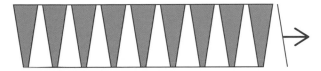

5. Make the border corners. Sew one white print wedge, two dark-color wedges, and one white print wedge all facing the same direction. Create four corner units. Sew a corner unit to both ends of two of the border strips.

6. To attach the borders to the quilt, find the center of the two border strips without corner units attached. Match up the centers to the center of two opposite sides of the pieced quilt top with the dark wedges pointing toward the quilt center. The wedge border strip will end 2" before either end of the quilt side. Carefully pin and sew the borders in place, starting and stopping sewing about 1½" away from the ends of the border strip (This is 3½" from the edge of the quilt).

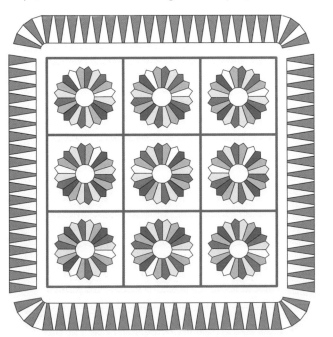

7. Center the two border strips with corner units to the remaining sides of the pieced quilt top and pin in place. Sew the borders to the quilt, starting and stopping about 2" before the end of the quilt edge. Leave the ends of the borders unattached.

8. Join the ends of the wedge corner units with the wedges at the end of the adjacent border strips. Press the seam allowances toward the dark wedges. All four corners should be connected, but unattached to the pieced quilt top.

9. Using a circle template or small plate as a guide, carefully trace and trim the four corners of the blue-gingham sashing to make rounded edges.

10. Carefully pin the curved border corners to the curved quilt edges. If the curves are not matching up perfectly, take in the seams slightly on the border wedges. Sew the border corner edges to the pieced quilt top. Press the seam allowances toward the blue-gingham sashing.

FINISHING THE QUILT

1. Cut and piece the backing fabric to create a backing that is at least 4" to 6" larger than the quilt-top measurements.

2. Prepare the quilt sandwich and machine or hand-quilt as desired (see page 154). Trim the edges.

3. Make bias binding from the red gingham fabric (see page 155). It is important to use bias binding for this quilt so that it fits smoothly around the curve of the corner edges. Bind the quilt as on page 156.

MODERN
DRESDEN PLATE

Shattered Dresden

DESIGNED, PIECED, AND QUILTED BY MARCI WARREN-ELMER

FINISHED DIMENSIONS 60½" wide x 76½" long

INSPIRATION

I love the shape of the Dresden wedge in its most traditional form but I wanted to incorporate it into a project that didn't involve any appliqué. Splitting the Dresden wedge into pieces creates a ton of negative space to do some dense quilting. It also allows the fabrics to shine. The color palette I used in this quilt was inspired by my love of the outdoors.

FABRIC

Yardages are based on 44"/45"-wide fabric.

Neutral background: 3¾ yards

Assorted solid scraps: Nine pieces approximately 8" x 10" (or nine ⅛-yard cuts)

Assorted print scraps: Nine pieces approximately 8" x 10" (or nine ⅛-yard cuts)

White or off-white: ½ yard

Coordinating binding print: ½ yard

Cotton fabric for backing: 4 yards

Batting: 2 yards (90" wide)

Fabric Notes

■ **Solid fabrics used in this project:** Riley Blake Solid (neutral background fabric), Kona Plum 1294, Kona Berry 1016, Kona Honey Dew 21, Kona Cactus 199, Kona Kiwi 1188, Kona Mango 192, Kona Flame 323, Kona Peacock 1282, Kona Cadet 1058, and Kona Snow 1339.

■ **Print fabrics used in this project:** Peach Herringbone – Sorbet Garden Henry Glass, Grass Architextures by Carolyn Friedlander, Plum Architextures by Carolyn Friedlander, Blue Architextures by Carolyn Friedlander, Blue Dot – Queen Street by Jennifer Paganelli, Purple – Outfoxed Purple Jewels by Lizzy House, Green Print – DS Quilts Sugar Creek/Winding Road, Lime Green Print – DS Quilts Sugar Creek/Winding Road, Orange Squiggle Stripe – Sweet Pea by Jackie Shapiro, Little Kita in Mineral Dust-Glimma by Lotta Jansdotter.

SUPPLIES

■ General Sewing Supplies (page 150)
■ EZ Quilting Tools Easy Dresden Quilt Tool Set #882700 by Darlene Zimmerman or template on page 142

■ **MARCI WARREN-ELMER**

Marci has always had a crafty side. When she was growing up, her mom was constantly working on a project and her grandma was an amazing seamstress. Despite (and because of) these sewing influences, she is a self-taught sewer. She began sewing in 2009 as a way to relieve stress from her 9 to 5 job and has found it the perfect way to balance her day job with her crafty side. Marci lives in Utah with her husband and two dogs. She enjoys hiking, traveling, and biking in her spare time.

CUTTING THE FABRIC

Use the EZ Quilting Tool or wedge template on page 142 to cut the wedges.

1. From the neutral background fabric, cut:

- Three 8" x width of fabric strips for Dresden wedges
    Sub-cut into 50 total 8"-Dresden wedges
- Ten 1¾" x 30" strips (used to separate the Dresden wedges)
- Six 2½" x 30" strips (used to separate the Dresden wedge blocks)
- Three 2½" x width of fabric; trim off the selvages (used for the center side borders)

- One 62" x width of fabric piece for the outer borders; trim off the selvages;
    Sub-cut lengthwise into four pieces:
        17½" x 61½" (right border)
        6½" x 61½" (left border)
        10" x 61" (top border)
        6½" x 61" (bottom border)

2. From the assorted solid fabrics, cut:

- Three 8" Dresden wedges from each of the nine solid fabrics, for a total of 27

3. From the assorted prints, cut:

- Two 8" Dresden wedges from each of the nine print fabrics, for a total of 18

4. From the white/off-white fabric, cut:

- Two 2½" x 38" strips
- Three 2½" x width of fabric strips; trim off the selvages

5. From the binding fabric, cut:

- Seven strips 2¼" x width of fabric; trim off the selvages

6. Optional: cut 2¼" x 2¼" squares of solid-colored fabrics to add rainbow pieces to the binding

SEWING INSTRUCTIONS

All seams are sewn right sides together using a ¼" seam allowance unless otherwise indicated.

Constructing the Dresden Wedge Strip Blocks

1. Align long edges of one solid-colored Dresden wedge and one neutral Dresden wedge with narrow Dresden end to wide Dresden end. Edges should be slightly offset so the pieces will match at the seam line. Sew pieces together, alternating colored wedge and neutral wedge. Continue sewing until you have ten neutral wedges and nine colored wedges sewn together.

2. Repeat step one to make a total of three solid-colored/neutral strips and two print/neutral strips. Press well.

3. Trim each Dresden wedge strip so they are rectangles measuring 30" x 8". Make sure the colorful Dresden wedges stay centered in the strip.

4. Using a ruler, cut a Dresden wedge strip lengthwise into three pieces: cut a 2½"-wide strip off the top of the Dresden wedge strip and cut a 2½"-wide strip off the bottom of the Dresden wedge strip. This leaves a 3"-wide strip from the middle.

5. Sew the bottom of the top wedge strip to a 30" x 1¾" strip of neutral fabric. Press seam allowances toward the neutral strip. Attach the top of the middle wedge strip to the other side of the neutral strip. Press seam allowances toward the neutral strip. Sew another 30" x 1¾" strip to the bottom of the middle wedge strip. Press seam allowances toward the neutral strip. Sew the top of the bottom wedge strip to the other side of the second neutral solid strip. Press the seam allowances toward the neutral strip. This Dresden wedge strip block now measures 30" x 9½".

6. Repeat steps 4–5 for the remaining solid and print Dresden wedge strips.

ASSEMBLING THE QUILT TOP

1. Join the Dresden wedge strip blocks with 2½" x 30" strips of neutral fabric. Sew a neutral strip on the bottom of a solid Dresden wedge strip block. Press seam allowances toward the neutral strip. Sew a print Dresden wedge strip block to the neutral strip. Repeat, alternating solid and print blocks. Once all five wedge strip blocks are sewn together, sew a 2½" x 30" strip of neutral fabric to the top and bottom of the unit.

2. Sew the three neutral background 2½" x width of fabric strips together end-to-end. Press the seams and cut into two 57½"-long strips. Sew these strips to the left and right sides of the unit.

3. Add the white (or off-white) inner borders. Sew the three white 2½" x width of fabric strips together end to end. Press seams and cut into two pieces: 2½" x 57½". Sew these pieces to the left and right sides of the Dresden wedge strips unit. Sew the two white 2½" x 38" strips to the top and bottom.

4. Add the outer border. Sew the 17½" x 61½" piece onto the right side; sew the 6½" x 61½" piece onto the left side. Press seams well. Square up the corners and trim any excess fabric. Sew the 10" x 61" piece onto the top and sew the 6½" x 61" piece onto the bottom. Square up the corners and trim any excess fabric. Press seams well.

FINISHING THE QUILT

1. Cut the backing fabric in half, trim the selvage edges off and sew long sides together. Press the seam well.

2. Prepare the quilt sandwich and machine or hand-quilt as desired (see page 153). Trim the edges.

3. Stitch the seven binding strips together end to end, forming one long strip. As an option, sew rainbow pieces of scraps into the binding. Press the strip in half lengthwise, with wrong sides together. Bind the quilt as on page 155.

Bear
Paw

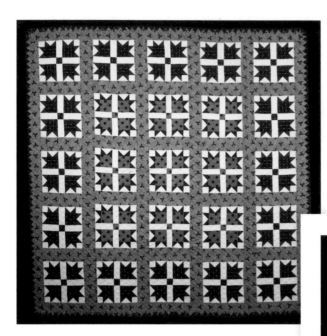

Drunkard's Bear Paw
Maker: A. Dunkle, Morrison's
Cover, Pennsylvania; Ca. 1865;
Cotton; 74" x 76";
Michigan State University
Museum #2007:107.7

Crow Foot in Mud Bear Paw
Maker: Sina R, Phillips
(Muskegon, MI); Ca. 1983;
Cotton, polyester; 72" x 80";
Michigan State University
Museum #6788.1

Bear Paw Quilt
Maker: unknown;
Ca. 1890-1910;
San Jose Museum
of Quilts and Textiles

BEAR PAW INSPIRATION

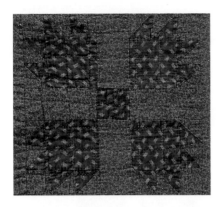

Just looking at some of the intricate patterns created by the Bear Paw block makes one realize how creative and talented our early quilters were in piecing together geometric shapes. This block of piercing geometric shapes is known by many names according to Barbara Brackman, including Bear Paw, Indian Trail, Forest Patch, Rambling Road, North Wind, and Irish Puzzle.* As people became more connected in the latter half of the 19th century through mail and newspapers, the sharing of quilt patterns followed suit—thus the wide variety of names. This certainly shows how regional quilt blocks were recognized and how the names of the blocks were often changed to support the environment of particular quilters, as well as the charitable causes for which the quilts might have been made. One such example is the quilt from Pennsylvania on the top left of the facing page. It's the color combination of pinks and browns that attracted me to A. Dunkle's Drunkard's Bear Paw. They are visually calming and sweet.

Darlene Zimmerman's Bear Paw quilt is traditional in pattern and color, but she added an attractive scallop border for design interest and to challenge her students. And, while Elisa Sims Albury's crib quilt cannot be mistaken for anything else but a Bear Paw, her use of negative space and her color palette makes this a very modern design.

*Pg. 180 #1354, *Encyclopedia of Pieced Quilt Patterns*, Complied by Barbara Brackman AQS

TRADITIONAL
BEAR PAW

A Long Winter's Night

DESIGNED BY DARLENE ZIMMERMAN AND QUILTED BY BARB SIMONS, STONE RIDGE QUILTING

FINISHED DIMENSIONS Approximately 66" wide x 84" long, with 6" blocks

FABRIC

Four different white/cream/tan prints: ⅝ yard of each for background

Red prints: 15 fat quarters

Brown prints: 15 fat quarters

Binding: ½ yard

Backing: 5 yards

Batting: Twin size

INSPIRATION

The name Bear Paw quilt brings to mind red flannel shirts, a cozy wood fire, hot chocolate and cold nights. Naturally, I chose the colors from this mental image—reds and browns—to make this not only a cozy quilt, but a rather masculine quilt as well. Snuggle in for a long winter's night!

SUPPLIES

- General Sewing Supplies (page 150)
- Simpli-EZ Quilting Tools Easy Scallop Tool #8823754A by Darlene Zimmerman or template on page 143

DARLENE ZIMMERMAN

A resident of rural Minnesota, Darlene is married, the mother of four children, and a grandmother to five. Her quilting career moved beyond designing and making quilts for family and friends to designing quilting tools for EZ Quilting (Simplicity Creative Group). She now has more than 30 quilting tools on the market. Darlene has also been busy designing 1930s reproduction fabric collections for Robert Kaufman Fabrics.

Not one to stop at designing tools and fabrics, Darlene has provided quilting inspiration and instruction for many quilters with her book series. She published four books with EZ Quilting (*Companions: Quilts and Miniatures; The Quilter's Kitchen; Calming the Storm;* and *Quilts to Come Home To*) and ten books with F + W Publications (*Quick Quilted Miniatures; Granny Quilts; Granny Quilts Décor!; Fat Quarter Small Quilts; The Quilter's Edge; The Complete Guide to Quilting; Quilts from Lavender Hill Farm; Fresh from the Clothesline; Quilt Finishes;* and *Quick Quilt Projects*).

Additionally, Darlene frequently publishes articles and patterns in quilt magazines, and self-publishes patterns under her company name of Needlings, Inc. Visit Darlene at www.feedsacklady.com.

ASSEMBLING THE BORDER

1. Alternating brown and red rectangles sew together on the long edges. Starting and ending with a brown print rectangle, sew 27 rectangles together for the top and bottom borders. The border seams can be pressed in either direction to alternate with the seam allowances in the body of the quilt. Decide the direction and then press the border seams.

 etc.

2. Match and pin each seam intersection between the top/bottom borders and the top/bottom quilt body. Stitch and press the seam allowances toward the borders.

3. Make two side borders of 36 pieced rectangles, starting with a brown rectangle and ending with a red rectangle. You will have a few rectangles left over. Press as described in step 1.

 etc.

4. Sew a red Bear Paw block to each end of the two side borders, making sure the paw is pointing to the outside. Sew the borders to the sides of the quilt; matching and pinning seam intersections as before. Press the seam allowances toward the borders.

FINISHING THE QUILT

1. Cut the backing in half, trim off the selvage on one long edge of the two pieces. Sew those trimmed edges together to make a backing approximately 80" x 90".

2. Layer the backing wrong side up, and the batting and the quilt top right side up. Baste then quilt as desired. Refer to page 153 for basting and quilting tips.

3. Before binding, mark wavy edges on the quilt with a chalk pencil using the Simpli-Ez Easy Scallop Tool or the template on page 143 set at 7" for the top and bottom edges and 7½" for the side edges. Leave the corners square. Baste on that marked line, either by hand or with a walking foot on the machine. This keeps the layers from stretching and shifting while the binding is sewn on. Do NOT cut on the marked line at this time.

4. Using the ½ yard of binding fabric, cut bias strips (at a 45-degree angle) 1¼" wide for a single bias binding. Join the binding ends with diagonal seams, and press seam allowances open.

5. Sew the binding to the quilt, using the basted marked line as a placement guide for the binding, and sewing a ¼" seam allowance below the marked line. Trim the batting, backing, and quilt top ¼" from the stitching line (ideally you will be cutting on the marked line after stitching the binding). No need to clip the curves.

6. Tuck the binding under ¼" on the back side of the quilt, stitching it down with matching thread.

MODERN
BEAR PAW

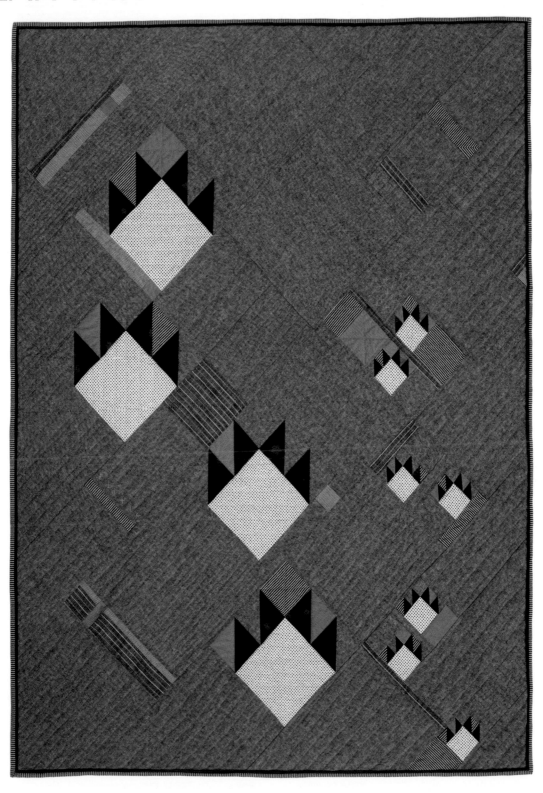

Berry Hunt

INSPIRATION

From the beginning, I knew I wanted to "deconstruct" the Bear Paw block. I played with several arrangements before selecting this one. I loved the concept of a "momma bear" and "baby bear" quilt. I've been increasingly drawn toward an indigo color palette, like quilts produced in the wa style of Japanese quilting. When designing this quilt, I kept thinking about what an urban hipster mom would like for her babe: something subtle, sophisticated, and gender-neutral. The subject matter reminds me of a favorite children's book, Blueberries for Sal, by Robert McCloskey, which tells the story of two "children" who get separated from their mothers. The yarn-dyed linen, chambray, and railroad stripe fabrics perfectly capture the colors of the book's illustrations.

DESIGNED, PIECED, AND QUILTED BY ELISA SIMS ALBURY

FINISHED DIMENSIONS 42½" wide x 56½" long

FABRIC

All fabrics provided by Robert Kaufman Company. Railroad denim is 57"-wide. If using different fabric, adjust yardage accordingly.

White dot: ¼ yard for bear paws (Mixmasters by Patrick Lose, APL-7585-181 Onyx)

Essex linen in navy: ½ yard for flange and bear toes (E014-1243 Navy)

Essex yarn-dyed linen: 3 yards for background (E064-1178 Indigo)

Railroad denim narrow stripe: ¼ yard for background (CXC-14110-62 Indigo)

Chambray: ¼ yard for background (SRK-14054-67 Denim)

Railroad denim poplin: ½ yard for background (CXC-13906-67 Denim)

Railroad denim stripe: ¾ yard for background and binding (CXC-14112-62 Indigo)

Quilter's linen dot: 2¾ yards for backing and bear toes (SRK-13631-62 Indigo)

Batting: 45" X 60" Crib size

SUPPLIES

- General Sewing Supplies (page 150)
- Wool or perle cotton for decorative stitching (if desired)

ELISA SIMS ALBURY

Elisa gave herself the gift of quilting one New Year's Eve resolution and has never looked back. For the past 14 years, she has been quilting and experimenting with numerous forms and techniques. It is her creative outlet, compared to the technical demands of her day job as a scientist. Elisa also worked as an editor for quilt magazines and pattern books, and recently started teaching classes on fabric-stash building and management, and liberated quilting techniques. She is an active member in her local guild, the Salt Lake Modern Quilt Guild.

Elisa considers herself a liberated quilter, choosing to create her own designs rather than work from patterns. She starts with a simple sketch, a word, a photograph, or a magazine page. She is a slow, process-driven quilter and her quilts evolve as she works. She believes a quilt will tell you what it needs, if you listen. Learn more about Elisa's projects, processes, and opinions on her blog www.stitchoutsidetheditch.com.

CUTTING THE FABRIC

1. BEAR PAW BLOCKS

From white dot for the paws, cut:
- One 6½" x width of fabric strip
   Sub-cut: Four 6½" x 6½" squares for large bear paw
- Seven 2½" x 2½" squares for small bear paw

From Essex linen in navy and/or quilter's linen dot and/or scraps as desired for paw toes, cut:
- One 4" x width of fabric strip
   Sub-cut: Eight 4" x 4" squares for large bear paw toes
- 14 2" x 2" squares for small bear paw toes

From background fabrics (or use a variety if desired), cut:
- Two 4" x width of Fabric strips
   Sub-cut: Eight 4" x 4" squares for large bear paw toes
- Four 3½" x 3½" squares for large bear paw
- 14 2" x 2" squares for small bear paw toes
- Seven 1½" x 1½" squares for small bear paw

2. BACKGROUND

The seaming in the background as well as inserts in the rows are designed to add interest and can be cut from a single fabric, a cohesive selection of yardage, or scraps. Many of the large pieces can be sub-divided with smaller pieces of other background fabrics to add even more interest. Include or eliminate as desired.

Because the background pieces are so many different sizes, use a "cut as you design" process. Here is a suggested list of cuts that you may alter during the design process.

From Essex yarn-dyed linen, cut:
- One 22½" x width of fabric strip and sub-cut to:
   One 22½" x 14½" rectangle
   One 19" x 12" rectangle
   One 19½" x 11½" rectangle
- Two 11" x width of fabric strips and sub-cut to:
   One 4½" x 11" rectangle
   One 6½" x 11" rectangle
   Two 8" x 11" rectangles
   One 11¼" x 11" rectangle
   One 11" x 11" square
- One 10½" x width of fabric strip and sub-cut to:
   One 4" x 10½" rectangle
   One 16" x 10½" rectangle
   One 10" x 16" rectangle

- Two 9½" x width of fabric strips and sub-cut to:
   One 2" x 9½" rectangle
   One 10½" x 9½" rectangle
   Two 16" x 9½" rectangles
   One 16½" x 9½" rectangle
   One 9" x 14" rectangle
- One 6½" x width of fabric strip and sub-cut to:
   One 20" x 6½" rectangle
- One 3½" x width of fabric strip and sub-cut to:
   One 2" x 3½" rectangle
   Two 2½" x 3½" rectangles
   One 3" x 3½" rectangle
   One 4½" x 3½" rectangle
   One 8" x 3½" rectangle

- Two 5½" x width of fabric strips and sub-cut to:
   One 1½" x 5½" rectangle
   One 2" x 5½" rectangle
   One 5¼" x 5½" rectangle
   One 8½" x 5½" rectangle
   One 12½" x 5½" rectangle
   One 16" x 5½" rectangle
   One 18" x 5½" rectangle
   One 5" x 1" rectangle
   One 5" x 15" rectangle

From railroad denim poplin, cut:
- One 11" x 1" rectangle
- One 11" x 2½" rectangle
- One 10½" x 2" rectangle
- One 10" x 1" rectangle
- Two 5½" x 1½" rectangles
- One 5½" x 5¼" rectangle
- One 2½" x 2½" square
- One 6" x 6" square

From railroad denim stripe, cut:
- One 5½" x 1¼" rectangle
- One 5½" x 1½" rectangle
- One 5½" x 2" rectangle
- One 3½" x 4" rectangle
- One 3½" x 5" rectangle

From railroad denim narrow stripe, cut:

- One 9½" x 1½" rectangle
- One 11" x 1" rectangle

From chambray, cut:

- One 3½" x 2" rectangle
- One 3½" x 5 ½" rectangle

3. FLANGE AND BINDING

From Essex linen in navy for flange, cut:

- Six 1" strips; trim the selvages

From railroad denim stripe for binding, cut:

- Five 2¼" strips; trim the selvages

SEWING INSTRUCTIONS

While there are many seams in this quilt, the horizontal rows are very forgiving. With the exception of piecing the bear paw blocks and bear paw sections, the pieces can easily shift from side to side. Don't worry about precisely lining up each paw in one row with the seams in the one above or below. This is an organic quilt.

All seams are sewn right sides together using a ¼" seam allowance unless otherwise indicated.

Assembling the Blocks

You'll assemble large and small bear paw blocks.

Large Bear Paw Blocks (4 blocks, finished size 9")

1. Draw a diagonal line on the eight 4" background squares.

2. Layer a background square on top of a 4" paw-toe square. Stitch ¼" on each side of the drawn line.

3. Cut on the drawn line to yield sixteen half-square triangle units. Press seam allowances toward the dark triangle.

4. Trim each square to 3½" x 3½".

5. Use these half-square triangle units, the four 6½" paw squares and the four 3½" background squares to assemble four large bear paw blocks as shown in the illustrations for the traditional bear paw quilt by Darlene Zimmerman (page 57). Press seam allowances toward the dark fabric.

Small Bear Paw Blocks (7 blocks, finished size 3")

1. Draw a diagonal line on the fourteen 2" background squares.

2. Layer a background square on top of a 2" paw-toe square. Stitch ¼" on each side of the drawn line.

3. Cut on the drawn line to yield 28 half-square triangle units. Press seam allowances toward the dark triangle.

4. Trim each square to 1½" x 1½".

5. Use these half-square triangle units, the seven 2½" paw squares and the seven 1½" background squares to assemble seven small bear paw blocks in the same way as for the large bear paw blocks.

ASSEMBLING THE QUILT TOP

1. Use the assembly illustration at right to assemble each row. Alter the individual pieces as desired. It is easiest to press away from the paws at this point. The end pieces for each row will finish with a jagged edge and will be trimmed when squaring the quilt. Be careful handling the quilt, as the cut bias edges will stretch easily.

2. Using the illustration, assemble the quilt top in numerical order as follows, section 1 to section 2 to section 3 to section 4, etc.

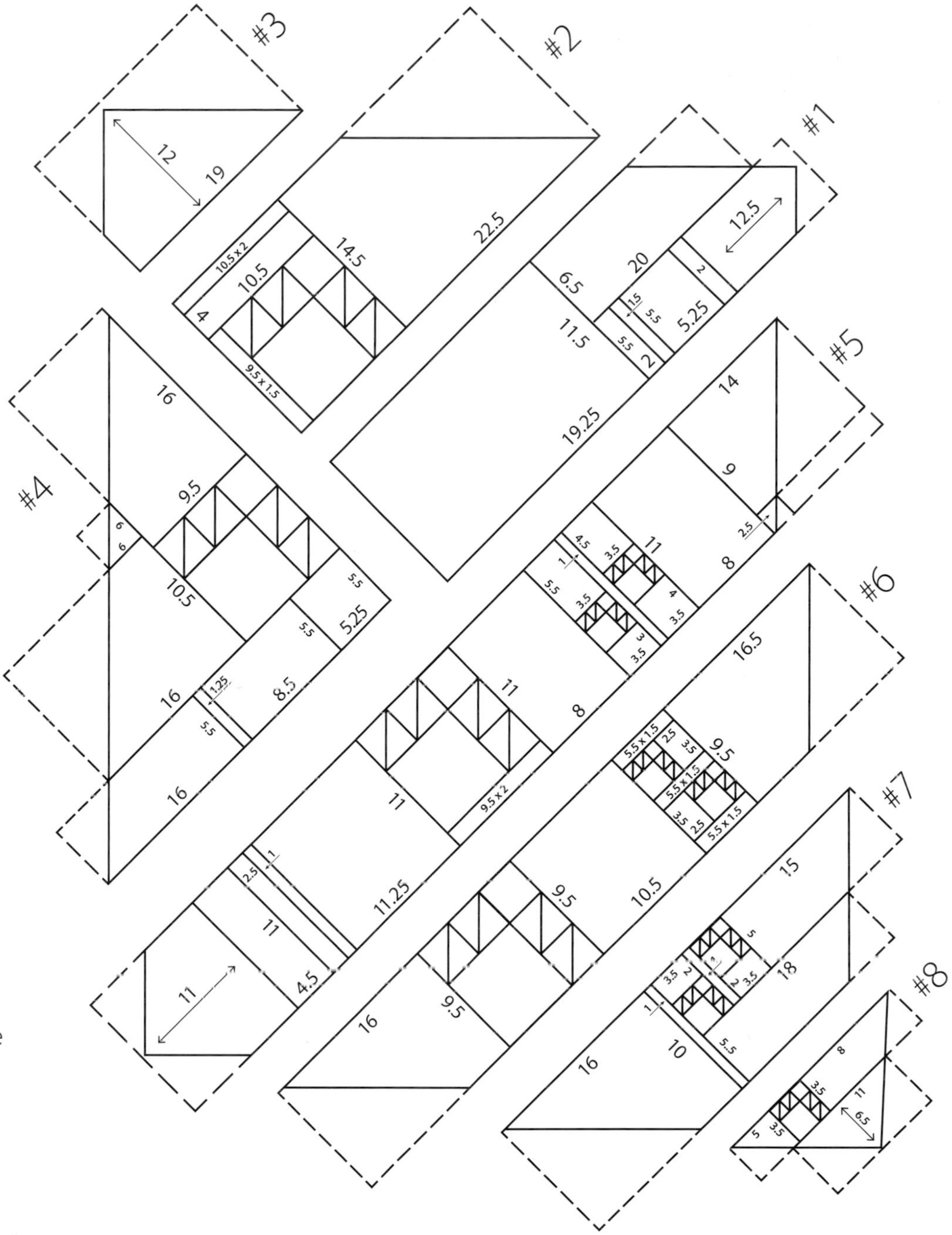

FINISHING THE QUILT

1. At this point, the quilt top has many pointed ends of the rectangles sticking out along the edges. Don't cut or trim until after quilting, when the quilt is squared up.

2. Cut and piece the backing fabric to create one that is at least 4" to 6" larger than the quilt top.

3. Prepare the quilt sandwich (see page 153).

4. Negative space is an excellent opportunity for thoughtful quilting. The quilt shown features straight-line quilting (in a variety of widths) stitched parallel to the rows, and perpendicularly for interest in several places. Stitching in the ditch around the paws makes them pop. Also add interest with hand quilting, using wool thread.

5. After quilting, square up the quilt to 42½" wide x 56½" long.

6. Sew the six flange strips together end-to-end with a diagonal seam. Press the flange in half along the length. Attach the flange by laying the prepared flange on top of the quilt sandwich, lining up the raw edges. Stitch ⅛" from the edge to secure.

7. Sew the binding strips together end-to-end and press in half along the length. Bind the edge of the quilt (see page 155).

Log Cabin

Log Cabin, Barn Raising
Member of the Lentz Family
(Lebanaon County, PA); Ca. 1875-1890;
Wool challis, hand-pieced and quilted;
New England Quilt Museum,
Lowell, MA; Lentz Family Log Cabin,
gift of the Binney Family, 1991.20;
Photo by Ken Burris

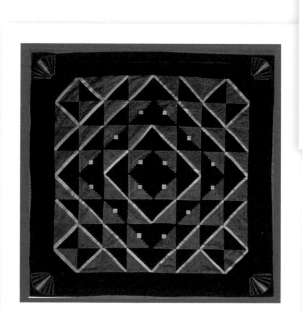

**Pineapple Quit,
Windmill Blades Log Cabin;**
Maker: unknown;
Ca. 1885-1910; Silk and velvet;
San Jose Museum of Quilts
and Textiles

Silk Log Cabin
Maker: anonymous; Ca. 1880-1890;
Silk, satin, brocade; hand-pieced, quilted.
and hand-embroidered; 61" x 61";
New England Quilt Museum, Lowell, MA,
Gift of Binney Family, 1991.21

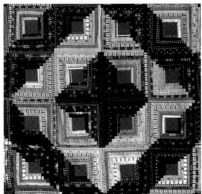

LOG CABIN INSPIRATION

The Log Cabin, along with the Double Wedding Ring, might be two of the most recognizable quilt patterns to the general public today. The Log Cabin pattern has been found in mosaic tiles, graphic illustrations, and apparel textiles throughout the centuries and in all parts of the world. It continues to be very popular among today's traditional and modern quilters and is also known as Log Patch, American Log Patchwork, and Colonial Block.* It probably owes its celebrity to the multitude of configurations that can be made with the use of solids, prints, and light/dark fabric combinations. Traditionally, its red center symbolizes the open hearth found in the center of many homes. Many of the early quilts were made from old clothing and pieced onto a thin backing foundation fabric in hopes of stabilizing the scraps. They were usually tied instead of quilted and were often made for farmhands and soldiers going off to war during the second half of the 19th century. The Log Cabin quilt was also one of the most popular quilt patterns that women made for fundraising. Interestingly, we can also see women from all walks of life first expressing their political voices through their traditional pastime of quilting.

Pat Sloan's quilt uses the Log Cabin pattern in a very traditional manner. At first glance, her palette seems more a contemporary choice, when actually it is fashioned after a quilt from the 1850s. Jacquie Gering's quilt has been stripped down to the core of the log cabin pattern. Her bold use of color and intricate diagonal quilting makes it particularly exciting.

*Pg. 38, #2573, Log Cabin, *Encyclopedia of Pieced Quilt Patterns*, compiled by Barbara Brackman AQS

TRADITIONAL
LOG CABIN

Cozy Time Log Cabin

INSPIRATION

When Michele asked me to design a traditional Log Cabin quilt, I was thrilled to work with this block. The Log Cabin block is one that so many of us learned to make when we first started. It is comfortable and beginner friendly. With the endless number of layouts, even seasoned quilters can make a Log Cabin quilt over and over again and never tire of it. The large center creates another design element that I find super exciting. On the back of the quilt, I added some of the Log Cabin blocks with a strip fabric. The reason? I had some test Log Cabin blocks and I didn't have enough flannel for the backing! Scrappy quilts are all about "making do" and this one sure does. Please send me a photo of your quilt; I'd love to see it!

DESIGNED BY PAT SLOAN, PIECING HELP BY ROBERTA MIGLIN, QUILTED BY CINDY DICKENSON OF PINKPAW & CO. (WWW.PINKPAW.COM).

FINISHED DIMENSIONS Approximately 60" wide x 80" long with 10" blocks

FABRIC

Yardages are based on 44"/45"-wide fabric, adjust as needed.

Red fabric 1: ½ yard for center squares

Red fabric 2: 1⅛ yards for center squares and binding

Other red fabric: 2 yards total quantity of a wide variety for the strips (see fabric notes)

Cream fabric: 2¼ yards total quantity of a wide variety for the strips (see fabric notes)

Black fabric: ¼ yard total quantity of a variety for the strips (see fabric notes)

Backing: 5 yards

Batting: Twin size

Fabric Notes

- This is a true scrap-buster project. I worked with my stash, using at least a dozen different red fabrics. I also added black strips in with the red. I love adding black to my projects.

- The cream fabrics are either tonal cream or cream with a red. Again, I used at least a dozen different fabrics. I kept them light enough so they wouldn't blend into the red; no medium tones.

- Since I owned some red flannel, I mixed it in with the cotton prints.

- When I trimmed off some of the pieces, I sewed the shorter strips together instead of throwing them out. This makes some interesting little places in the blocks.

PAT SLOAN

Pat is a designer, author, lecturer, and with her weekly radio show, is the *Voice of Quilting*. Sewing since she was a child and quilting for more than 20 years, Pat eventually looked to her craft to start her own business. She started to teach quilt making to others and then turned her skills to pattern designing. In 2000, Pat and her husband Gregg formed a design and publishing company called Pat Sloan & Co. In addition to designing and publishing her work, they now travel around the country teaching and showing her quilts to quilt guilds and quilt shops. Pat has also had her designs published in many national magazines, has

written 30 books on quilting, and has designed several lines of fabric for P&B Textiles and Moda.

When Pat took her passion to the Internet, she built several quilt communities, and five years ago started a weekly *All Quilting* radio/podcast (www.creativetalknetwork.com). You can hear her interview quilt historians, designers, and authors from around the world. Five years of podcasts are available for download. Sign up for Pat Sloan's email newsletter at www.patsloan.com, read her blog, check out her free pattern page, join her online quilt group, and follow her on Facebook, Twitter, and Instagram.

MODERN
LOG CABIN

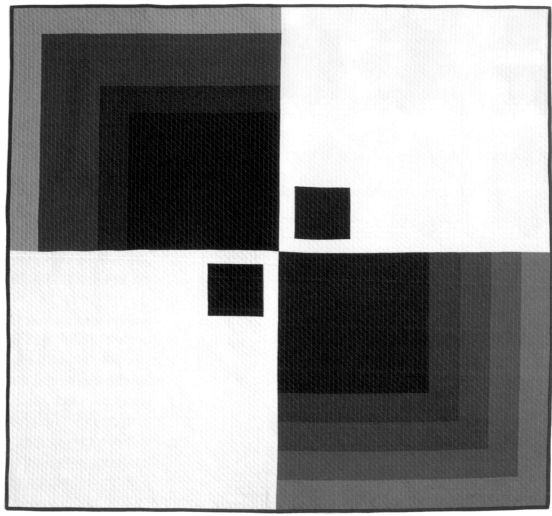

Hot Flash

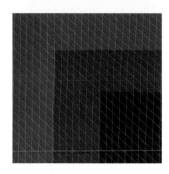

INSPIRATION

I've been focusing on the concept of minimalism in my work, so I wanted to go minimal with this design. I love the Half Log Cabin (or chevron block), so I chose that since Log Cabin was my assignment. The colors and the "feeling" of the quilt were inspired by my struggle of dealing with, living with, and hating the hot flashes that have been consuming me lately. The tagline for this quilt is, "My husband wears socks and a sweatshirt in the summer!" I love the graphic simplicity of this quilt and how heat radiates from it, while at the same time the stark white feels cold, which is how I'd love to feel.

DESIGNED, PIECED, AND QUILTED BY JACQUIE GERING

FINISHED DIMENSIONS Approximately 54" wide x 54" long

FABRIC

Yardages are based on 44"/45"-wide fabric.

Orange fabrics, colors ranging from light to dark with the A fabric being the darkest, E being the lightest

A – ⅔ yard
B – fat eighth (9" x 22")
C – ⅛ yard
D – ¼ yard
E – ¼ yard

Pink fabrics, colors ranging from light to dark with the F fabric being the darkest, J being the lightest

F – ⅔ yard
G – fat eighth (9" x 22")
H – ⅛ yard
I – ¼ yard
J – ¼ yard

White background fabric (K):
1¼ yards

Backing fabric: 3⅜ yards

Binding fabric: ½ yard

Low-loft cotton batting:
66" x 66"

SUPPLIES

- General Sewing Supplies (see page 150)
- 24" clear acrylic ruler

JACQUIE GERING

Jacquie is a passionate modern quilt maker and designer. She is known for her innovative out-of-the-box designs, striking message quilts, and unique style. Her work has been featured in both national and international publications, as well as several books. *Quilting Modern: Techniques and Projects for Improvisational Quilts* is her first book, published by Interweave Press in 2012. Jacquie is a leader in the modern quilting community and is a member of the Chicago Modern Quilt Guild. She is the former president of the Kansas City Modern Quilt Guild, and on the Board of Directors of the Modern Quilt Guild. She blogs and shares her quilting knowledge on her popular blog, Tallgrass Prairie Studio (tallgrassprairiestudio.blogspot.com) and lives in Chicago with her husband and black lab, Bruno.

CUTTING THE FABRIC

Refer to Hot Flash structure diagram on page 75 and measurements listed below.

1. Orange fabrics cut:

- A Fabric
  A1 - 15½" x 15½"
  A2 - 6" x 6"
- B Fabric
  B1 - 3½" x 15½"
  B2 – 3½" x 18½"
- C Fabric
  C1 – 3½" x 18½"
  C2 – 3½" x 21½"
- D Fabric
  D1 – 3½" x 21½"
  D2 – 3½" x 24½"
- E Fabric
  E1 – 3½" x 24½"
  E2 – 3½" x 27½"

2. Pink fabrics cut:

- F Fabric
  F1 - 15½" x 15½"
  F2 - 6" x 6"
- G Fabric
  G1 – 3½" x 15½"
  G2 – 3½" x 18½"
- H Fabric
  H1 – 3½" x 18½"
  H2 – 3½" x 21½"
- I Fabric
  I1 – 3½" x 21½"
  I2 – 3½" x 24½"
- J Fabric
  J1 – 3½" x 24½"
  J2 – 3½" x 27½"

3. White background fabric (K) cut:

- K1 – Two 2" x 6"
- K2 – Two 2" x 7½"
- K3 – Two 7½" x 20½"
- K4 – Two 20½" x 27½"

4. Binding fabric cut:

- Six 2¼" x width of fabric strips; trim off the selvages

SEWING INSTRUCTIONS

All seams are sewn right sides together using a ¼" seam allowance unless otherwise indicated. Press seams open.

Constructing the Hot Flash Blocks

This quilt consists of two blocks: Block A, a half log cabin or chevron block, and Block B.

Making Block A

Make two, one in each color way. Refer to the illustration and follow the steps below.

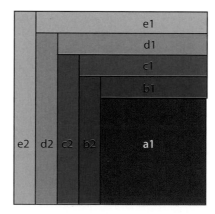

1. Place a pin at the top of A1. This is a compass pin to remind you which side of A1 is the top.

2. Sew B1 to the top of A1. Sew B2 to the left side of the A1/B1 section, making sure A1 is at the top.

3. Sew C1 to the top of the A1/B1/B2 section. Then sew C2 to the left side of the new section.

4. Sew D1 to the top of the A1/B1/B2/C1/C2 section. Then sew D2 to the left side of the new section.

5. Sew E1 to the top of the A1/B1/B2/C1/C2/D1/D2 section. Then sew E2 to the left side of the new section to complete Block A.

6. Repeat the process outlined in steps 1–5 to make another Block A in the pink color way using the F, G, H, I and J pieces.

Block B

Make two, using the dark orange and dark pink 6" squares. Refer to the illustration and follow the steps below.

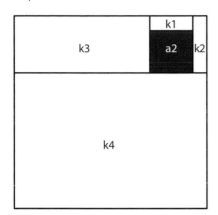

1. Sew K1 to the top of A2. Sew K 2 to the right side of the A2/K1 section, making sure K1 is at the top.

2. Sew K3 to the left side of the A2/K1/K2 section.

3. Sew K4 to the bottom of the A2/K1/K2/K3 section to complete Block B.

4. Repeat the process outlined in steps 1–3 to make the second Block B using the F2 piece.

ASSEMBLING THE QUILT TOP

1. Place the four blocks on the design wall as shown in the structure diagram.

2. Sew the orange Block A to the left side of Block B (with the pink square) to complete Row 1.

3. Sew Block B (with the orange square) to the left side of the pink Block A to Complete Row 2.

4. Sew Row 1 to Row 2 to complete the quilt top.

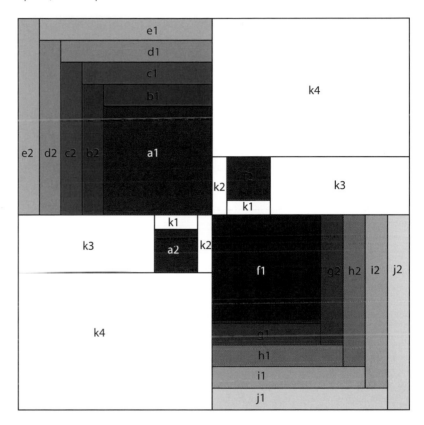

FINISHING THE QUILT

1. Join the six binding strips together using diagonal seams to create a continuous binding strip. Press the strip in half lengthwise with wrong sides together (see page 155 for binding tips).

2. Cut and piece the backing fabric to measure approximately 60" x 60".

3. Lay the backing wrong side up on a flat surface securing the edges. Place the batting on the backing and then center the quilt top on the batting, right side up. Baste (see page 153).

4. Quilt as desired (see page 153). Square the quilt and attach the binding to finish the quilt (see page 155).

Nine Patch

Pinwheel and Nine-Patch Quilt
Donor: Bruce Berman; Maker: unknown;
Ca. 1910; Cotton; San Jose Museum of
Quilts and Textiles

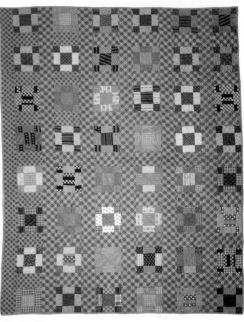

Nine Patch
Maker unknown (provenance unknown);
Ca. 1875; 69.5" x 90.5"; Michigan State
University Museum #2007:107.10

Nine Patch Variation Quilt
Donor: Bruce Berman; Maker: unknown;
Ca. 1870; Cotton; San Jose Museum of
Quilts and Textiles

Nine Patch Quilt
Donor: Bruce Berman; Maker: Rosalee Farmer;
Ca. 1995; 104" x 73"; Purchased at African-
American co-op in Mississippi; San Jose
Museum of Quilts and Textiles

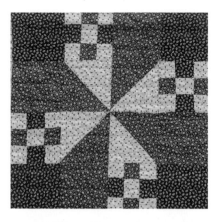

NINE PATCH
INSPIRATION

▣ The simplicity of the Nine Patch pattern seems to appeal to most beginner quilters because of its straight lines and basic blocks. Many of the early Nine Patch quilts were made and used for strictly utilitarian purposes. However, it also appears to be a pattern that quilters seem to take liberties with. It was the first quilt I made and I know I had the confidence to play with the sashing and borders because the blocks were so simple to make. During my research, I was occasionally stumped when looking at Nine Patch quilts—sometimes you have to really hunt for the pattern. The basic pattern can also be found as filler blocks between stars, flying geese, and more intricate configurations of triangles and unusual patterns.

The arrangement of shirting fabrics that appear in the top right quilt from the late 1800s is a good example of using fabrics to create interest and visual appeal. For the first time, material was being manufactured at a surprising rate in the United States, which made yard goods more widely available and gave women who were making quilts from old, used clothing many more options.

■ I love that Kaari Meng chose to make a Disappearing Nine Patch as the traditional offering. Her design is done in the spirit that the Nine Patch pattern evoked in me when I first studied the historical quilts: interesting, puzzling, and frankly just plain old amazing. Bonnie Bus's stripped down pattern and very bold color choices play upon the negative space and remind us of the humble beginnings of this traditional quilt, in the most modern of ways.

TRADITIONAL
NINE PATCH

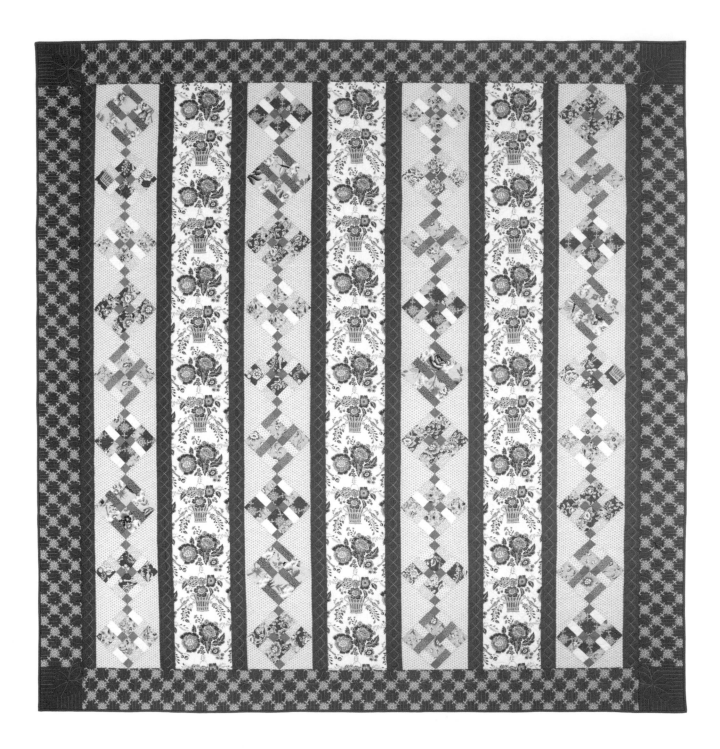

Le Bouquet Français

DESIGNED BY KAARI MENG OF FRENCH GENERAL AND QUILTED BY PENELOPE TUCKER

FINISHED DIMENSIONS Approximately 85" wide x 89" long

FABRIC

All fabrics used in the sample are from Le Bouquet Français by French General. Yardages are based on 44"/45"-wide fabric (42" usable fabric). Adjust yardage for different widths, as needed.

6 assorted large prints:
¼ yard each for blocks (Fabric A)

12 assorted small prints:
⅛ yard each for blocks (Fabrics B & C)

Solid blue: ⅓ yard for blocks (Center fabric)

Small print: 2¼ yards for the setting triangles

Solid red: 3½ yards for narrow vertical strips (includes 1 yard for bias binding)

Basket print: 2½ yards for the vertical floral strips

Red floral: 2½ yards for the outer border

Backing: 8½ yards

Batting: Queen size

INSPIRATION

I was thrilled to be assigned the traditional Nine Patch quilt for this book. I decided to sew a simple variation of the Nine Patch and make the Disappearing Nine Patch. This is a great pattern for a scrap quilt and is one of those designs that looks more difficult to make than it actually is. The Disappearing Nine Patch incorporates any number of squares, as long as that number is divisible by nine. I made the quilt out of fabrics from French General's Spring 2014 collection, Le Bouquet Français.

SUPPLIES

- General Sewing Supplies (page 150)
- 12" square acrylic ruler (for trimming the blocks)
- 24" acrylic ruler
- 90-degree quarter-square triangle ruler

KAARI MENG

Kaari Meng was raised in a large creative family in Southern California. Encouraged from an early age to be independent and create something unique, Kaari found her niche designing jewelry for Anthropologie. Sixteen years ago, with the help of family and friends, she opened French General (www.frenchgeneral.com), a vintage craft workshop in Los Angeles. Since then, Kaari discovered the countryside of France, the flea markets, and her true passion—textiles!

For the past six years, she has designed quilting fabric and patterns for Moda based on French General's collection of early 19th century florals and stripes. Inspired by the past, Kaari has also written a handful of books on vintage crafts, sewing, and entertaining. And, every summer, she continues to take women to France to live in a chateau and find their inner Frenchwoman. To learn more about Kaari, visit www.the-art-of-craft.com.

CUTTING THE FABRIC

These directions assume that a directional fabric is being used, as shown in the sample quilt.

1. BLOCKS

■ From Fabric A—Assorted large prints, cut:

Two 3¼" x width of fabric strips from each of the six large prints

Sub-cut each fabric into 24 3¼" x 3¼" squares, for a total of 144 squares

■ From Fabric B & C—Assorted small prints, cut:

One 3¼" x width of fabric strip from each of the 12 small prints

Sub-cut each fabric into 12 3¼" x 3¼" squares, for a total of 144 squares

■ From solid blue center fabric, cut:

Three 3 ¼" x width of fabric strips

Sub-cut into 36 3¼" x 3¼" squares

2. SETTING TRIANGLES

■ From small print fabric, cut:

Four 4¾" x length of fabric strips.

Sub-cut into 32 left-facing and 32 right-facing triangles using the quarter-square triangle ruler

One 5⅛" x length of fabric strip

Sub-cut into eight 5⅛" x 5⅛" squares

■ Cut four of the squares diagonally from the upper left corner

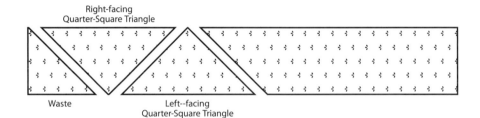

Right-facing Quarter-Square Triangle

Waste

Left--facing Quarter-Square Triangle

to the lower right corner to form eight half-square triangles. Cut the remaining four squares diagonally in the opposite direction (from upper right corner to lower left corner) to form eight mirrored half-square triangles.

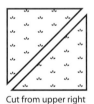

Cut from upper right to lower left

Cut from upper left to lower right

3. NARROW VERTICAL STRIPS

■ From solid red fabric, cut:

Eight 2 ½" x 77" strips on the lengthwise grain of fabric

Four 6 ½" x 6 ½" squares

Set aside the rest of the solid red fabric for the bias binding

4. VERTICAL FLORAL STRIPS

■ From basket print fabric, cut on the lengthwise grain of fabric, centering the basket motif:

Three 8" x 77" strips

5. BORDER

■ From Red Floral Fabric, cut on the lengthwise grain of fabric, centering the lattice motif:

Two 6 ½" x 73" strips

Two 6 ½" x 77" strips

6. BINDING

■ From solid red fabric, cut:

Bias binding from one yard of fabric to make at least 350" of 2¼"-wide bias binding (see page 155). More fabric may be required if you choose to make a wider binding.

SEWING INSTRUCTIONS

All seams are sewn right sides together using a ¼" seam allowance unless otherwise indicated.

Assembling the Blocks

Final block size is 6½" including seam allowances.

1. The blocks begin with a traditional nine-patch block consisting of four 3¼" Fabric A squares, two 3¼" Fabric B squares, two 3¼" Fabric C squares and one 3¼" blue center square.

- Arrange the four Fabric A squares in each corner, two Fabric B squares in the center of the top and bottom rows, two Fabric C squares on each side of the middle row and one blue center square in the middle. Sew the squares together in each row. Then, sew the rows together to make a traditional nine-patch block that measures 8¼" including seam allowance.

- Make six nine-patch blocks with each Fabric A, B, & C combination for a total of 36 blocks.

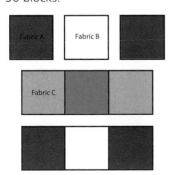

2. Using your ruler, cut each nine-patch block in half through the center vertically and horizontal, creating four uneven four-patch blocks.

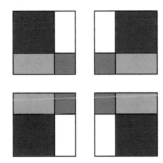

3. Trim the four blocks to 3½" square, leaving the blue square to measure 1¼".

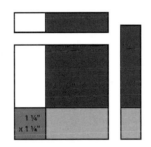

4. Arrange the four 3½" squares so that two opposite blue squares are pointing toward the middle and the remaining two are pointing toward the corners. Sew the blocks together in each row. Sew the rows together to complete the block. Your new block should measure 6½".

- Make six blocks with each Fabric A, B, & C combination for a total of 36 blocks.

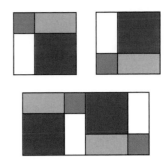

Assembling the Vertical Rows of Blocks

1. Arrange nine blocks on point in a vertical row so that top and bottom corners contain a blue square.

2. Place eight left-facing quarter-square triangles between the blocks on the left and eight right-facing quarter-square triangles between the blocks on the right.

3. Place a left-facing half-square triangle on the top and bottom of the left side of the vertical row and a right-facing half-square triangle on the top and bottom of the right side of the vertical row.

4. Sew the triangles to each side of each block to create diagonal rows. Sew the diagonal rows together to create a vertical strip of blocks that measures 9" x 77".

5. Make three more vertical strips in the same manner, for a total of four vertical strips of blocks. Each strip measures 9" x 77".

ASSEMBLING THE QUILT

1. Sew a 2½" x 77" solid red strip to each side of the vertical block strips.

2. Place an 8" x 77" basket floral strip between each of the four vertical block strips and sew together to complete the quilt center. Your quilt should now measure 73" x 77".

3. Sew a 6½" x 77" border strip to each side of the quilt.

4. Sew a 6½" solid red square to each end of the two 6½" x 73" border strips. Sew these borders to the top and bottom of the quilt.

5. Your quilt should now measure 85" x 89".

FINISHING THE QUILT

1. Cut the backing fabric into three pieces, and trim off the selvages. Sew the three pieces together on the long sides. Press the seams.

2. Lay the backing wrong side up and place the batting on top with raw edges aligned. Center the quilt top, right side up, on top of the batting. Secure all three layers together by basting or with safety pins (see page 153).

3. Quilt as desired. Trim the edges to square up the quilt. Apply the binding around the perimeter of the quilt (see page 155).

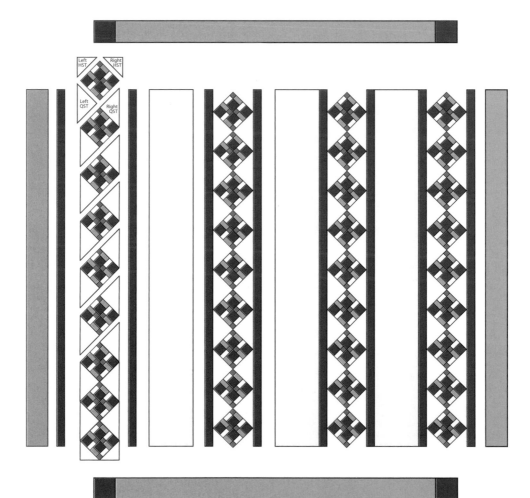

MODERN
NINE PATCH

Oscillation

DESIGNED BY BONNIE BUS AND QUILTED BY KARI RUDISALE OF EATON RAPIDS, MI

FINISHED DIMENSIONS Approximately 72" wide x 94" long

FABRIC

All yardages are based on 44"/45"-wide fabrics. This quilt would also work well with scraps or your favorite designer line of fabric. If using scraps, you will need approximately four yards of fabric (total) for squares and rectangles.

White solid: 2¼ yards (to be cut lengthwise)

11 medium solids: ½ yard each:
yellow, orange, red, bright pink, purple, marine blue, teal, turquoise, medium olive, Kelly green, light Kelly green

3 very light solids:
1 fat quarter each: lavender, blue, yellow-green

Backing fabric: 5½ yards

Batting: Queen size

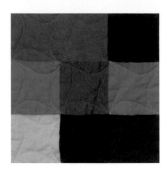

INSPIRATION

When Michele asked me if I could make a modern version using the Nine-Patch, this quilt popped into my head. Amazing. Maybe it was waiting there all the time and just waiting to be cut and sewn. This quilt was fun to make, and once I finished, it reminded me of the wave on an oscilloscope.

SUPPLIES

■ General Sewing Supplies (page 150)

BONNIE BUS

Like many others, Bonnie has been quilting since the 1970s. She always loved to be creative, but not by throwing out quilting's traditional past. The modern quilt movement has helped her intertwine tradition with new concepts. Bonnie is a teacher, author, artist and a devoted quilter. She lives in Lansing, Michigan, with her husband.

CUTTING THE FABRIC

There will be a few extra 3" x 3" squares and 3" x 4" rectangles. Use the squares in the rainbow effect in the top and bottom borders. The extra rectangles can be used in another project.

1. For the horizontal sashing, cut lengthwise from white solid fabric:
- Four 3½" x 72½" strips
- Three 2½" x 72½" strips

2. For nine-patch block with 3" x 3" (finished size) squares, cut:
- From each medium solid: 18 3½" x 3½" squares
- From each light solid: Four 3½" x 3½" squares
- From white solid: 16 6½" x 9½" rectangles

3. For nine-patch blocks with 3" x 4" (finished size) rectangles, cut:
- From each medium solid: 16 3½" x 4½" rectangles
- From each light solid: Two 3½" x 4½" rectangles
- From white solid: 16 8½" x 9½" rectangles

SEWING INSTRUCTIONS

All seams are sewn right sides together using a ¼" seam allowance unless otherwise indicated.

Assembling the Blocks

Make 16 square nine-patch blocks using the 3½" x 3½" squares.

1. Lay out each block of nine squares on a flat area such as a table or design wall. The squares should be placed three across and three down to make a nine-patch. Choose colors at random or arrange to please yourself. Include one light solid in at least twelve of the blocks.

2. Sew these squares into a nine-patch. Sew the first two squares together in the top row, then sew the third square to the two previously sewn squares to make a row. Repeat with the next two rows of squares. Sew the rows together by sewing the top row to the middle row, then the bottom row to the middle row.

3. These square nine-patch blocks measure 9½" by 9½".

Make 16 rectangle nine-patch blocks using the 3½" x 4½" rectangles.

1. Lay out each block of nine rectangles on a flat area such as a table or design wall. The rectangles should be placed three across and three down to make a nine-patch. Choose colors at random or arrange to please yourself. Include one light solid in at least twelve of the blocks. Be sure that all rectangles are placed with the 3" side at top.

2. Sew these rectangles into a nine-patch. Sew the first two rectangles together in the top row and then sew the third rectangle to the two previously sewn rectangles to make a row. Repeat with the next two rows of rectangles. Sew the rows together by sewing the top row to the middle row, then the bottom row to the middle row.

3. These rectangle nine-patch blocks measure 9½" x 12½".

ASSEMBLING THE QUILT TOP

Sew the nine-patch blocks to the white rectangles.

1. Sew a 6½" x 9½" white rectangle to any side of the 9½" square nine-patch blocks. These blocks now measure 9½" x 15½".

2. Using the 9½" x 12½" rectangle nine-patch blocks, sew the 8½" x 9½" white rectangle onto the 9½" side of the block. These blocks now measure 9½" x 20½".

Sew the blocks into rows.

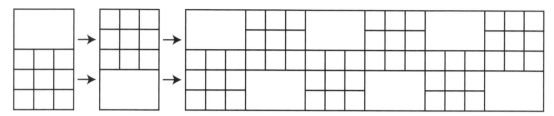

1. Using the 9½" x 15½" square nine-patch blocks, sew eight blocks side-by-side, being sure to alternate the white rectangle from top to bottom for the entire row. Repeat with the second group of eight square nine-patch blocks. Both rows measure 15½" x 72½".

2. Repeat the previous step using the 9½" x 20½" rectangle nine-patch blocks. Both of these rows measure 20½" x 72½".

Sew the rows together.

1. Sew a 2½" x 72½" white strip to one side of a square nine-patch row.

2. Sew the unstitched side of the white strip to a rectangle nine-patch row to form a combination row of square and rectangle nine-patches.

3. Repeat steps 1 and 2 to make a second combination row.

4. Sew a 2½" x 72½" white strip to one of the combination rows.

5. Sew the two combination rows together using the unstitched side of the white strip. Be sure the white strip is between a square nine-patch row and a rectangle nine-patch row.

Make the borders.

1. Sew twelve of the leftover 3½" squares in a row to make a color rainbow as follows: yellow, orange, red, pink, purple, blue, teal, medium olive, turquoise, Kelly green, light Kelly green and yellow-green.

2. Repeat the rainbow sequence so there are two rainbows in each border row.

3. Make two border rows, each measuring 3½" x 72½".

4. Sew a 3½" x 72½" white strip to both sides of each border rainbow row.

Attach the borders to the quilt top.

1. Sew the borders to the top and bottom of the quilt. Remember that the the quilt rows should be horizontal, as shown at right.

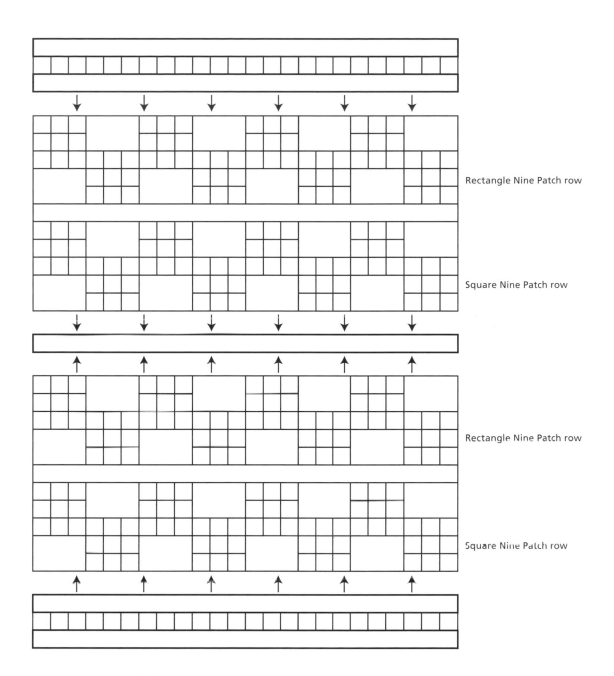

Rectangle Nine Patch row

Square Nine Patch row

Rectangle Nine Patch row

Square Nine Patch row

FINISHING THE QUILT

1. Cut and piece the backing fabric to create a backing that is at least 4" to 6" larger than the quilt-top measurements.

2. Prepare the quilt sandwich and machine- or hand-quilt as desired (see page 153).

3. Bind the quilt as on page 159.

Hexagon

 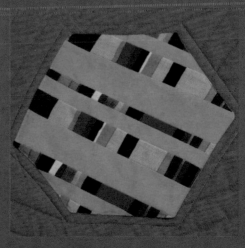

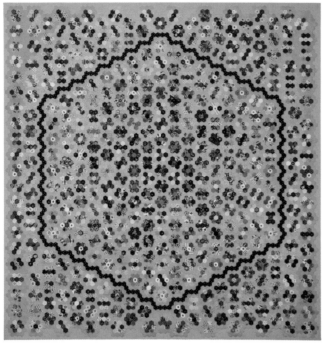

Grandmothers Flower Garden
Donated by Sarah Gummersall;
Maker: Mary Tayloe Lloyd Key
(probably Maryland); Ca. 1840; 90" x 84";
Cotton, chintz and paper pieced;
San Jose Museum of Quilts and Textiles

Hexagon
Collection of Linda Pumphrey;
Maker: unknown; Ca. last quarter
of the 1800s; Velvet and silk

Hexagon Appliqué Quilt
Maker: Mattie Nicewonger-Musgrove;
Ca. 1890s; Cotton; trapunto, appliqué;
San Jose Museum of Quilts and Textiles

HEXAGON INSPIRATION

GRANDMOTHER'S FLOWER GARDEN

■ According to family history of the donor of the quilt at the top of the facing page, Sarah Gummersall, this Grandmother's Flower Garden quilt top was pieced by Mary Tayloe Lloyd Key, wife of Francis Scott Key, for Alice, the tenth of their eleven children. It is said that the pieces were lined with family letters.

The Hexagon is a shape that continues to make an appearance in fashion, graphic illustrations, advertising, and of course quilting. The smallest of hexies were often paper-pieced, a process that has recently regained popularity as the go-to project for traveling quilters. Typically the paper is removed before completing the quilt. However, vintage or antique quilts that have been paper-pieced (or well-labeled) can often provide clues regarding by whom, where, and when these quilts were made. The papers (newspapers, magazine articles, and even love letters) can usually be studied in quilt tops that have not been finished with a filler and backing yet. Many of the Hexagon quilts that we see from the 1800s are made with silk fabric in an allover random pattern, more than likely an influence of English quilters. Known throughout quilting history as the Hexagon, Honeycomb, Mosaic, Century Poor Boy, Friendship Quilt, and Hit or Miss,* the Hexagon quilt will obviously continue to be a popular pattern.

■ Linda Pumphrey hand-pieced her traditional wall hanging with a black background that boldly sets off the colorful flower clusters. Her inspiration was an antique quilt from her personal collection. Leslie Tucker Jenison's modern quilt also has a dark background, but it sets off her scrappy hexagon and octagon shapes in a very large format.

*Pg. 30, #160, Hexagon, *Encyclopedia of Pieced Quilt Patterns*, complied by Barbara Brackman AQS

TRADITIONAL
HEXAGON

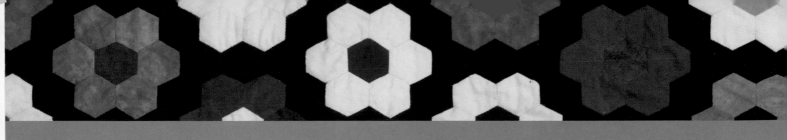

Grandmother's Flower Garden

INSPIRATION

The beauty and simplicity of the design work exhibited in antique Hexagon quilts inspired me to recreate them using modern tools and fabrics.

DESIGNED, PIECED AND QUILTED BY LINDA PUMPHREY

FINISHED DIMENSIONS Approximately 49" wide x 49" long

FABRIC

Yardages are based on 44"/45"-wide fabric.

12 Assorted Prints:

⅓ yard of each of the following colors for blocks and piano key border: light yellow, light cream, medium cream, medium orange, dark orange, light pink, light bue, dark blue, light brown, medium brown, dark brown, medium gray

Black: 2¼ yards for sashing blocks, inner border and binding

Backing: 3½ yards

Batting: 60" x 60"

SUPPLIES

- General Sewing Supplies (page 150)
- Cardstock paper (for templates)
- Hexagon templates on page 145

- Optional Accuquilt GO! Dies in the following sizes:
    GO! English Paper Piecing
     Hexagon 1" Finished 55422
    GO! 2½" Strip Cutter 55014
    GO! 1¼" Strip Cutter 55109
    GO! 4½" Strip Cutter 55054

LINDA PUMPHREY

Linda Pumphrey is a quilter and quilt historian, who also enjoys a career in the quilting industry. Linda says, "Quilts are much like my job: full of color with different patterns and made of layers. Quilting has been a family passion for at least five generations." She serves on several national boards, including the International Quilt Study Center and Museum and the Quilt Alliance. She is also an award-winning quilter. For twenty years, Linda was the National Sales Manager for Mountain Mist, the original inventor of filler products and quilt battings. While at Mountain Mist, Linda acted as curator of the Historical Mountain Mist Corporate Quilt Collection and was instrumental in bringing the collection to Nebraska.

In 2009, Linda joined the AccuQuilt team, located in Omaha, Nebraska. She is currently the Global Sales manager, and oversees sales strategies for both new and existing products. She describes this as her "dream job," because it involves both travel and quilting.

MODERN
HEXAGON

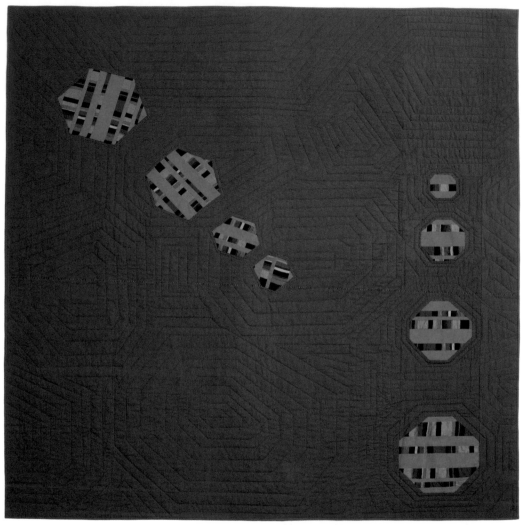

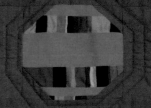

Octadelic and Hexalicious

BY LESLIE TUCKER JENISON AND QUILTED BY DANIELLE WILKES

FINISHED DIMENSIONS Approximately 54" wide x 60" long

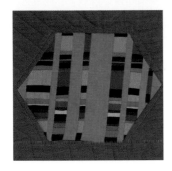

INSPIRATION

Let's face it. I have never seen a quilt I didn't love! I am smitten with the modern quilt aesthetic because the quilts honor the tradition of creating pieced, "usable" quilts, yet add a fresh approach to the colors and method of construction. I love piecing Hexagons and personally own quite a number of vintage Grandmother's Flower Garden quilts. It is with that background that I challenged myself to figure out a method of creating hexagon shapes with relatively simple machine piecing. The result is a fun, easy set of variable sized hexagons that is positively "hexalicious."

FABRIC

Yardages are based on 44"/45"-wide fabric.

Stripe or bold graphic print: ½ yard

Coordinating solid fabric: ¾ yard

Gray background fabric: 3½ yards to be cut lengthwise

Backing: 3½ yards

Binding: ½ yard

Batting: Twin size

SUPPLIES

- General Sewing Supplies (see page 150)
- Templates on page 145
- Freezer paper for hexagon templates
- Monofilament thread for appliqué (optional)

CUTTING THE FABRIC

1. From the striped or graphic print fabric, cut:
- Two 1" x width of fabric strips
- Two 1¼" x width of fabric strips
- Two 1½" x width of fabric strips
- Two 2" x width of fabric strips

2. From the solid fabric, cut:
- Two 1" x width of fabric strips
- Two 1¼" x width of fabric strips
- Two 1½" x width of fabric strips
- Two 2" x width of fabric strips

The remainder of this fabric will be cut when making the hexagons.

LESLIE TUCKER JENISON

Leslie Tucker Jenison is an award-winning artist who works primarily on the quilted surface. Surface design, using dye and paint, are integral components of her work, which has been shown internationally and has been featured in numerous publications. Leslie serves on the board of the Quilt Alliance and belongs to numerous quilt-focused organizations. She is one-half of the curating-teaching duo that represents *Dinner At Eight Artists*. Leslie teaches quilt and mixed media workshops nationwide. She enjoys photography, reading, gardening, traveling, and is a pilot with multi-engine and instrument ratings. When on the ground, she considers herself to be a pretty decent cook. Leslie is married and has three daughters, all of whom are artists. For more info, visit www.leslietuckerjenison.com.

3. From the solid gray background fabric, cut:

- Two pieces lengthwise:
  41" x 60½"
  5½" x 60½"
- From the remainder of the fabric, cut:
  For the octagon corners:
    Four 1½" x 1½" squares
    Four 2¼" x 2¼" squares
    Four 3" x 3" squares
    Four 3½" x 3½" squares
- For the pieced octagon block panels:
  Two 3½" x 3" rectangles
  Two 2½" x 5" rectangles
  Two 1½" x 7" rectangles
- For the interval panels between the octagons:
  One 21½" x 9" rectangle
  One 3" x 9" rectangle
  One 5" x 9" rectangle
  One 7" x 9" rectangle
  One 4" x 9" rectangle

SEWING INSTRUCTIONS

All seams are sewn right sides together using a ¼" seam allowance unless otherwise indicated. Press seams open.

Constructing the Octagon Blocks

1. Sew all of the striped fabric strips and the solid strips together in your own arrangement, alternating between solids and stripes. Press seam allowances open. The resulting pieced strip should measure approximately 15½" wide x width of fabric.

> **TIP** *Use a short stitch length to prevent these seams from separating when cutting the octagons and hexagons.*

2. From the pieced strip, select visually interesting segments and cut the following four squares (that will then be used to make the octagons): 9" x 9", 7" x 7", 5" x 5", and 3" x 3". Save the remaining strip-pieced fabric for the hexagons.

3. Each octagon features four gray squares, one in each corner. Finger press each gray square diagonally to assist with placement and stitching.

 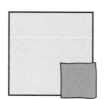

4. Place a 1½" gray square on each corner of a 3"-strip pieced square so that the gray extends ¼" beyond the edge of the strip-pieced corners. This extra fabric allowance assures that the corner, once stitched and flipped, will extend outward to complete the square (which includes the pieced octagon).

5. Stitch a diagonal seam just inside the fold line in each of the gray squares. Check the overlap prior to trimming the seam allowance to assure the fold will reach the corner. It's OK if the overlap is larger than the square as it will be squared up later.

6. Trim the seam allowance of the strip-pieced corner and the gray fabric to ¼" seam allowance and press the corner outward.

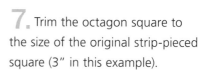

7. Trim the octagon square to the size of the original strip-pieced square (3" in this example).

8. Repeat steps 3 to 7 for each size block. The 5" strip-pieced square uses the 2¼" gray squares. The 7" strip-pieced square uses the 3" gray squares. The 9" strip-pieced square uses the 3½" gray squares.

9. You should now have four octagons set into squares that measure 3", 5", 7" and 9".

Constructing the Octagon Block Panels

1. To the 3" octagon block, sew a 3½" x 3" gray rectangle to each side. Press seam allowances toward the gray rectangles. This panel measures 3" x 9".

2. To the 5" octagon block, sew a 2½" x 5" gray rectangle to each side. Press seam allowances toward the gray rectangles. This panel measures 5" x 9".

3. To the 7" octagon block, sew a 1½" x 7" gray rectangle to each side. Press seam allowances toward the gray rectangles. This panel measures 7" x 9".

Constructing the Octagon Panel Stack

1. Lay out the octagon block panels and the interval panels as follows:
- 21½" x 9" interval panel
- 3" x 9" octagon block panel
- 3" x 9" interval panel
- 5" x 9" octagon block panel
- 5" x 9" interval panel
- 7" x 9" octagon block panel
- 7" x 9" interval panel
- 9" x 9" octagon block panel
- 4" x 9" interval panel

2. Sew all panels together in the order they're laid out. Press all seam allowances toward the gray panels. This octagon panel stack measures 9" x 60½".

Constructing the Hexagons

Use the remainder of the strip-pieced fabric to make the hexagons.

1. Make freezer paper templates (see page 145) for each of the four hexagon sizes: 2", 2½", 4", and 5".

2. Layer the strip-pieced fabric on top of the remainder of the solid fabric. Select visually interesting segments and press the four hexagon templates onto the fabric, shiny side down. Cut both fabrics at the same time ¼" larger than the template (for the seam allowance).

3. Place the solid and pieced hexagons right sides together and sew a ¼" seam around the outside edges, leaving one side open for turning. Remove the template.

4. Trim the seam allowances at each point.

5. Turn the hexagons right side out. Gently push the points out. Press the hexagon well. Fold the open edges inside and press.

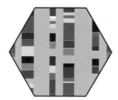

ASSEMBLING THE QUILT TOP

1. Sew the 5½" x 60½" gray rectangle to the right of the octagon panel stack.

2. Sew the 41" x 60½" gray rectangle to the left.

3. Press seam allowances toward the gray rectangles.

4. Pin the hexagons on top of the quilt so they appear to "tumble" across the surface.

5. Using monofilament thread or a coordinating thread color, sew each hexagon to the quilt surface close to hexagon edge.

> **TIP** *If desired, carefully trim away the fabric under the appliquéd hexagons to allow the batting to puff up under the shapes.*

FINISHING THE QUILT

1. For the quilt back, cut the backing fabric in half. Remove the selvages and sew the two pieces together along the long edges.

2. Prepare the quilt sandwich and machine- or hand-quilt as desired (see page 153).

3. Bind the quilt as on page 155.

Yo-Yo

Yo-Yo Quilt
Collection of Wendy Catch Reed;
Maker: unknown (CT);
Ca. 1952 for a wedding present;
Over 5,000 cotton yo-yos

Yo-Yo Quilt
Collection of Michele Muska;
Maker: Unknown; probably
Southern New England;
Ca. late 1930s to early 1940s;
93" x 110"; Cotton feed sack

Yo-Yo Coverlet
Maker: Tille Shelley;
Ca. 1930; Chiffon, no backing;
sized for twin bed;
San Jose Museum of Quilts
and Textiles

YO-YO INSPIRATION

The quilt at the center of the facing page is a typical representation of the Yo-Yo style in time, construction, and fabric. The 2,016 yo-yos are constructed mostly of cotton prints from feed sacks (at left, below) and recycled clothing. My mom found it at a yard sale, stuffed into a large garbage bag. The quilt was in excellent condition, so she scooped it right up for me for only $8.00 (more recently appraised at $500.00). The quilter had never really finished the quilt since there were several yo-yos sewn together and ready to add on to it. After making slight repairs and washing this more than 80-year-old quilt, the solids were very bright!

Yo-Yo quilts began to appear in the 1920s and remained popular through the 1930s and 1940s. Many women made the small scrappy circles from feed sacks. Agriculture feed and food grain companies put their product in bags that were made from printed cotton to encourage women, particularly the wives of farmers, to purchase their goods. Women were becoming more mobile and working away from the home, but many of them still felt the need to carry handwork with them and yo-yos fit the bill. It has also been suggested that the popularity of the toy yo-yo and its arrival in the U.S. during the 1930s could have added to the love of this quilt pattern. Yo-Yo quilts are also referred to as Puffs, Bed of Roses, Heirloom Pillow, Bon Bon, Yorkshire Daisy, Puff Ball, Suffolk Puffs, Pinwheel, Rosette, and Powder Puff.*

■ I chose to make and piece the yo-yos in my Child's Play quilt in a very traditional manner and appliquéd it to a solid and simply quilted background. This is meant as a shout out to the women of the past who wanted to show off their handiwork. In Monica Solorio-Snow's version, the juxtaposition of the bright and darkly colored yo-yos give her quilt a modern aesthetic. Her seemingly random, yet carefully positioned yo-yos also add a bit of whimsical freedom.

*Pg. 34, #194, Yo Yo; *Encyclopedia of Pieced Quilt Patterns*, Complied by Barbara Brackman AQS

TRADITIONAL
YO-YO

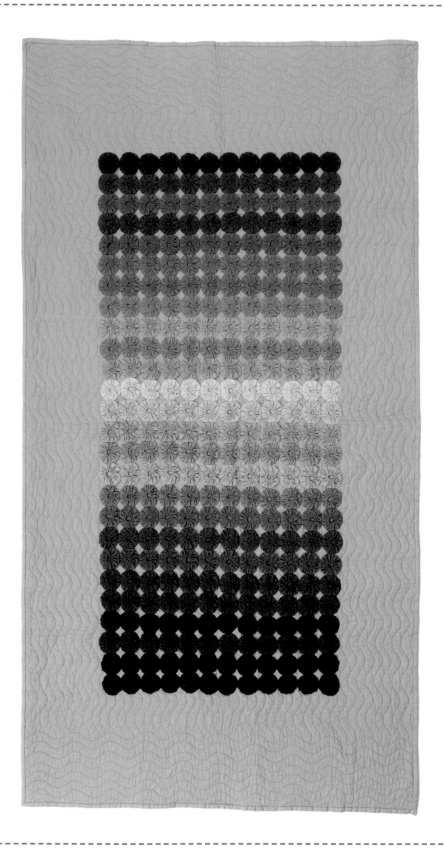

Child's Play

DESIGNED BY MICHELE MUSKA, QUILTED BY SHELLY PAGLIAI OF PRAIRIE MOON QUILTS, AND CIRCLES CUT BY MY SON, LOGAN NEE

FINISHED DIMENSIONS Approximately 40" wide x 80" long

FABRIC

I used fat quarter bundles from Robert Kaufman Kona Solids in True Blue Colorstory and Grecian Waters Colorstory for the yo-yos. For the quilt-top base, backing, and binding, I used Kona Solid in Iron Grey. Feel free to use scraps or any fabrics that you choose. Yardages are based on 44"/45"-wide fabric.

Solid colors: 27 fat quarters for yo-yos

Neutral solid: 5 yards for quilt top base and backing

Binding: ½ yard in color of your choice

Batting: slightly larger than 40" wide x 80" long

INSPIRATION

I've loved making Yo-Yo quilts for many years: I've stuffed them, beaded them, and tufted them. But I was especially excited when I took on the traditional Yo-Yo, and felt I should explore my love of color. Using 27 colors of Kona Solid Fabrics in rows of 12 brought back wonderful memories of my college painting days.

When I started designing my Yo-Yo quilt, I imagined a long quilt stretching the full length of my queen-size couch with all the little ones in my family lined up underneath to watch a favorite movie. I literally saw their tiny fingers tracing the circles and the spaces in between.

Like many Yo-Yo quilts from the 30s and 40s, my quilt has a solid background. I took the concept a bit further by having the base fabric quilted to strengthen the quilt and assure its longevity.

SUPPLIES

- General Sewing Supplies (page 150)
- 5" circle dye cutter for Accuquilt GO! OR 5" Yo-Yo template provided on page 147

CUTTING THE FABRIC

1. From the base and backing fabric, cut:

- Two 44"-wide x 84"-long pieces

2. Using the 5" template on page 147, from each of the 27 solid fabric fat quarters, cut:

- Twelve 5" circles for a total of 324 circles

> **TIP** Since many of my colors were similar, I put the circles of each color in a small bag and numbered the bag in the order that I had already decided. I returned each finished set of yo-yos to the numbered bag after they were sewn.

SEWING INSTRUCTIONS

All seams are sewn right sides together using a ¼" seam allowance unless otherwise indicated.

Making the Quilt

1. First make a 40" x 80" whole cloth quilt sandwich using the base and backing fabric with the batting between (see page 153).

2. Quilt with an overall design as desired (see page 153). (Shelly Pagliai quilted the quilt shown with wavy lines.)

3. Prepare the binding and bind the edges (see page 155) before adding the yo-yo unit.

Making the Yo-Yo Unit

Sew each circle into a yo-yo with a 2½" finished diameter.

1. Fold over the fabric edge of each circle ¼" to the wrong side of the fabric.

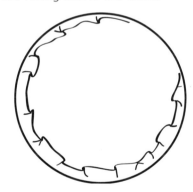

2. Hand-stitch a small evenly spaced running stitch with needle and thread around the entire circle.

3. Gently pull the thread to gather the disk into a circular puff. Flatten the circular puff and knot the end of the thread into place. Cut off the thread tail being careful not to cut the gathering stitches.

Sewing the Yo-Yos Together

1. Draw a line through the center on the backside of each yo-yo circle with your marking pencil. Draw a second line perpendicular to the first line.

2. Line up the same color yo-yos in a row, using the marked guidelines on the back. Sew all twelve yo-yos of the same color together by hand (with a whipstitch from the backside).

3. Line up the yo-yo rows in order of color preference using the guidelines on the back. Sew together by hand with a whipstitch from the backside.

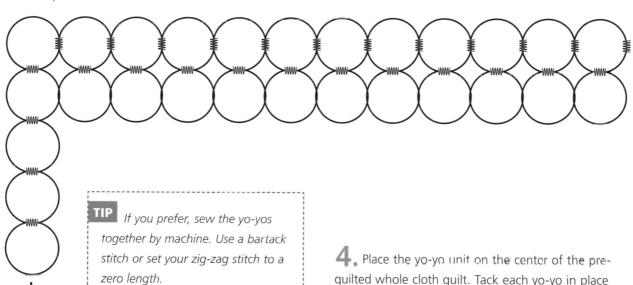

> **TIP** *If you prefer, sew the yo-yos together by machine. Use a bartack stitch or set your zig-zag stitch to a zero length.*

4. Place the yo-yo unit on the center of the pre-quilted whole cloth quilt. Tack each yo-yo in place by hand.

MODERN
YO-YO

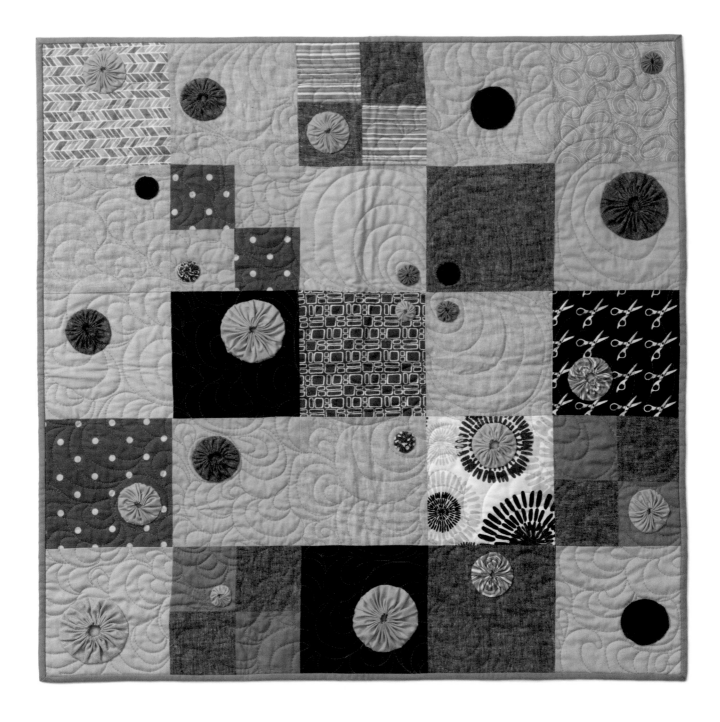

Yo!

INSPIRATION

There is zero quilting in my family background, so I had to create my own quilting memories and education. Alex Anderson on HGTV was my private teacher. Just Alex, my VHS machine, and me.

Quilts, fabrics, and patterns by Darlene Zimmerman were my connection to a past that didn't exist for me otherwise. It is because of Darlene that I have a love of all things 1930s. Traditional quilts from that time period make my love of modern quilts bloom. As a first-generation American, quilting is what makes me feel connected to all the good things in American history.

Yo! is a modern twist on a traditional Yo-Yo quilt, using all solid fabrics and one tiny little pop of a print that says, "YO! Look at me!"

■ MONICA SOLORIO-SNOW

As a native Californian living on the gray, damp North Oregon coast, Monica created sunshiny days with fabric, quilting, and sewing. Quilting turned from a way of coping with the weather into a full-blown love affair with all things fabric and "making." Those dark, rainy Oregon days became gifts that allowed Monica to stay inside and sew up some happiness. A little bit of making her own sunshine has evolved into fabric collections: the first with Lecien Fabrics of Japan, and Sew Yummy with Cloud 9 Fabrics, released in 2014. Many of Monica's quilting and sewing patterns can be found in collaborative books, *Better Homes & Gardens* publications, and magazines. Monica also self-publishes patterns and tutorials through her blog and shop at www.monicasolorio.com and www.thehappyzombie.com blog.

DESIGNED, PIECED, AND QUILTED BY MONICA SOLORIO-SNOW

FINISHED DIMENSIONS Approximately 30" wide x 30" long

FABRIC

All fabrics are 44"/45"-wide, 100% premium quilting cottons. I used assorted neutrals including a "pop color" of citron, but you can play around with the fabric colors to make it your own. Start with a 6½" square of print fabric that sings to you, then build around it and use it as your color guide.

Print fabric: One 6½" square

Flax: One fat quarter

Citron: One fat quarter

Black: One fat quarter

Light gray: One fat quarter

Medium gray: ⅛ yard

Dark gray: ⅓ yard

Backing and Binding: 1⅓ yard

Batting: 1 yard low-loft natural fiber batting

SUPPLIES

- General Sewing Supplies (see page 150)
- Yo-yo templates (page 146–147)

Flying
Geese

Flying Geese
Maker: Barbara Parsons Cartier
(Enfield, CT); Ca. 2013;
Cotton and batiks

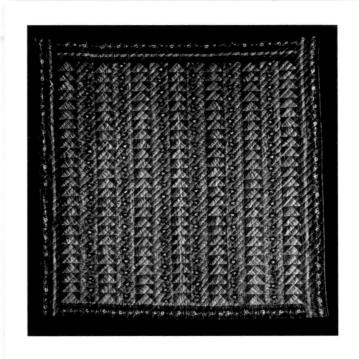

Flying Geese
Maker: unknown;
Probably New England
or Pennsylvania;
Ca. 1840-1860; 86" x 88";
Cotton with cotton filling;
Michigan State University
Museum #6521.1

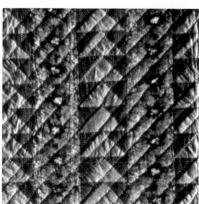

FLYING GEESE INSPIRATION

Wild Goose Chase, Birds in Flight, Wild Geese Flying, or Flying Geese* are what this particular pattern has been lovingly referred to throughout time. The large triangle represents the goose and the two smaller triangles are the sky. The Flying Geese pattern has often been paired with one or more different patterns to make up one quilt. It has also always been a popular choice for borders and sashing, or to frame out center medallion blocks. Depending on how you configure the blocks and position the fabric, the pattern can look very different. You can even see triangles chasing each other in circles.

Jackie Kunkel has chosen 1930s prints for her traditional pattern. The white background gives it a very fresh look, while the sweet overall floral quilting pattern gives it a traditional feel. Megan Frock's quilt uses the negative space to accentuate the bold chevrons that are made by configuring the Flying Geese blocks into the chevron shapes. Both quilts use the negative space to their advantage, but with very different visual results.

*Pg. 82, #480, Flying Geese; *Encyclopedia of Pieced Quilt Patterns,* Complied by Barbara Brackman, AQS

Homeward Bound

DESIGNED, PIECED AND QUILTED BY JACKIE KUNKEL, CANTON VILLAGE QUILT WORKS

FINISHED DIMENSIONS Approximately 63" wide x 82" long

FABRIC

Yardages are based on 44"/45"-wide fabric; adjust as needed.

White solid: 4 yards

A variety of 1930s prints: 2 yards total

Batting: Twin size

Backing: 4½ yards

SUPPLIES

- General Sewing Supplies (page 150)

CUTTING THE FABRIC

1. From the white fabric, cut:

- Seventeen 3⅞" x width of fabric strips
    Sub-cut into (164) 3⅞" x 3⅞" squares
- Thirteen 4" x width of fabric strips; trim off the selvages
- Two 6½" x 28½" strips
- Two 6½" x 15½" strips
- One 7¾" x 7¾" square

2. From the 1930s print fabrics, cut:

- Eight 7¼" x width of fabric strips
    Sub-cut into forty-one 7¼" x 7¼" squares
- One 7¾" x 7¾" square

INSPIRATION

One of my favorite blocks is Flying Geese, in all shapes and forms. Either alone or combined with other patchwork blocks, the Flying Geese make any quilt sing. In this particular traditional design, a simple setting was best and, of course, a collection of 1930s prints brings the tradition to life.

JACKIE KUNKEL

Jackie Kunkel has been a quilter for over 20 years: in business for thirteen years, designing for magazines for four years, and has taught classes for as long as she can remember. Jackie began her business as a long-arm quilter and now owns her own online quilt shop, Canton Village Quilt Works. Jackie is one of Judy Niemeyer's Nationally Certified Teachers and her online shop is a Judy Niemeyer Certified Shop. The process to become a

Certified Teacher is involved, but according to Jackie, worth every second. Now, Jackie teaches and travels to share her love of Judy's techniques and methods.

Jackie is an avid quilting blogger, and has been producing a podcast, *Jackie's Quilting Chronicles,* which can be found on iTunes. She coordinated a quilt show at the New England Air Museum for the past three years, as well. To find out more, visit www.cvquiltworks.com.

MODERN
FLYING GEESE

Haiku Crib Quilt

INSPIRATION

The Haiku crib quilt is a simple and modern approach to the traditional Flying Geese block: subtle enough to please a variety of mama's, yet intriguing enough to catch even baby's tiny eyes.

DESIGNED AND PIECED BY MEGAN FROCK,
QUILTED BY BEV JONES OF SEW SWEET QUILT SHOP

FINISHED DIMENSIONS Approximately 49" wide x 61 ½" long

FABRIC

Yardages are based on 44"/45"-wide fabric.

Print for block 1: One fat quarter

Print for block 2: One fat quarter

Two different prints for block 3: ½ yard each

Solid for background and blocks: 2½ yards

Binding: ½ yard

Backing: 3½ yards

Batting: Twin size

SUPPLIES

■ General Sewing Supplies (page 150)

Note: Please read through all of the instructions before getting started

MEGAN FROCK

Megan studied mixed media painting and street art, but soon after college was introduced to the world of quilting and has never looked back. Her style has been noted as a mixture of urban, modern, and vintage all rolled up in a sweet southern package. Megan is new to the quilting industry, but is quickly making strides with many publications, including being the cover girl for *Generation Q* magazine. Her first book, *The Hand Embroidered Haven* (published by F + W Media), is sure to awaken your hand-stitching senses. For more info, visit www.downtownhousewife.com.

CUTTING THE FABRIC

1. For the blocks:

- From one fat quarter (block 1), cut:
  Two 7¼" x 7¼" squares (peak)
- From second fat quarter (block 2), cut:
  Nine 3⅞" x 3⅞" squares (outside of peak)
- From each of the two half-yard prints
  (label as fabric 3a and fabric 3b for block 3), cut:
  Three 7¼" x 7¼" squares (peak)
  11 3⅞" x 3⅞" squares (outside of peak)
- From solid fabric, cut:
  One 3⅞" x width of fabric strip
  Sub-cut Eight 3⅞" x 3⅞" squares
  (block 1—outside of peaks)
  One 7¼" x width of fabric strip
  Sub-cut Three 7¼" x 7¼" squares
  (block 2—peaks)
  Two 6½" x width of fabric strips
  Sub cut 17 3½" x 6½" rectangles
  (blocks 1 and 2)

2. For the background:

Because the background pieces are so many different
sizes, either cut them as you sew or label them with
their size as you cut.

- From solid fabric, cut:
  Nine 6½" x width of fabric strips
  Sub-cut these strips into the following lengths:
  One of each:
  33½", 31½", 22½", 20½", 19½", 12½", 11",
  9½", 8½", 7½", 5½", 5", 2½"
  Two of each:
  24½", 10½"
  Three 3½"
  11 6½" x 6½" squares

3. For the binding, cut:

- Six 2½" x width of fabric strips; trim off
  the selvages

SEWING INSTRUCTIONS

All seams are sewn right sides together using a ¼" seam
allowance unless otherwise indicated. Press the seams
open or to one side as you go.

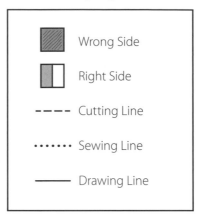

Constructing the Flying Geese Blocks

All flying geese units are the same size and will be
pieced using the same diagram; the only difference is
reversing the solid and the prints. The 7¼" squares form
the peak of the flying geese units and the 3⅞" squares
form the outside triangles of the flying geese units.
One 7¼" square plus four 3⅞" squares yield four
flying geese units.

Organize and lay out the fabrics to make the flying geese blocks:

- Eight of block 1 using two 7¼" squares of fat
  quarter print 1 (peak) and eight 3⅞" squares of solid
  (outside).
- Nine of block 2 using three 7¼" squares of solid
  (peak) and nine 3⅞" squares of fat quarter print
  #2 (outside).
- Twenty of flying geese units for block 3 using the
  two different half-yard prints, one in reverse of
  the other. Make ten flying geese units using three
  7¼" squares of fabric 3a (peak) and 11 3⅞" squares
  of fabric 3b (outside). Reverse the fabrics
  to make ten more flying geese units using three
  7¼" squares of fabric 3b (peak) and 11 3⅞" squares
  of fabric 3a (outside).

CREATING THE FLYING GEESE BLOCKS

1. Place one 7¼" square right side up. Next, gather two 3⅞" squares. Place one in each corner, right side down and diagonally across from each other. Pin in place.

2. Using a ruler, draw a diagonal line from corner to corner across the middle of both small squares.

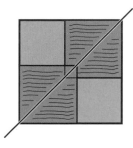

3. Sew a ¼" seam down each side of the drawn line.

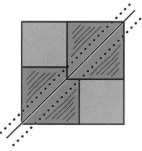

4. Cut directly on the drawn line to make two new pieces. Press the seam allowances open.

Press open.

5. Pin one 3⅞" square right side down in the corner of one of the new pieces and draw a diagonal line across it.

6. As you did before, sew a ¼" seam down each side of the line.

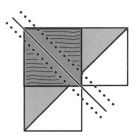

7. Cut directly on the drawn line and press the seam allowance open. Square up the blocks to 3½" x 6½" rectangles. This completes two flying geese blocks.

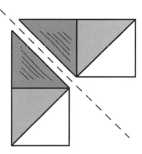

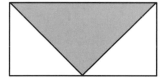

8. Repeat steps 5–7 for the second piece, which will yield two more flying geese blocks.

9. Repeat steps 1–8 to complete all of the flying geese for the quilt.

NOTE: You will have some extra flying geese pieces for your scrap basket.

ASSEMBLING BLOCKS

Each final block will measure 6½" x 6½".

1. For blocks 1 and 2, simply stitch one 3½" x 6½" solid to one flying geese unit, lining up the 6½" sides. For block 1, place the peak toward the solid. For block 2, place the peak toward the solid on four blocks and face the peak away on five blocks.

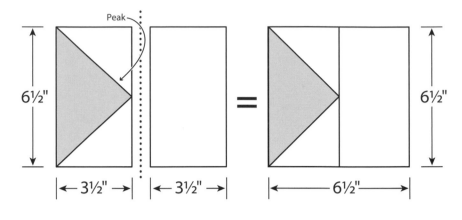

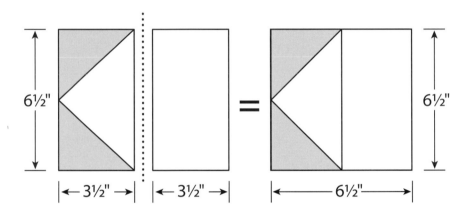

2. For block 3, stitch one of each of the two different flying geese units together at the 6½" sides. Make sure the center forms an arrow shape.

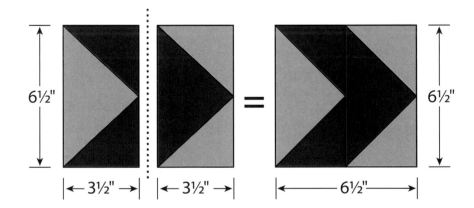

PIECING THE QUILT

1. Using a design wall, layout the geese and background solid pieces in eight columns as shown in the assembly diagram. Pay attention to the direction of the flying geese blocks. Stitch each column as shown, pressing seams as you go.

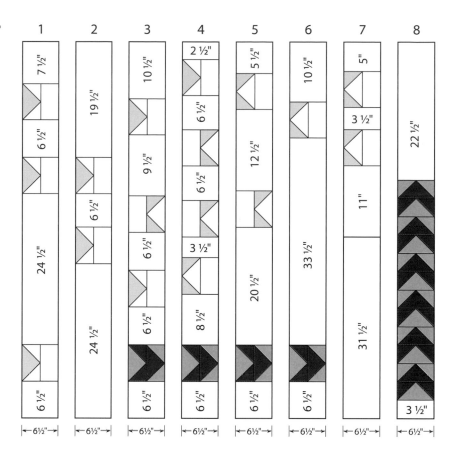

2. When all the columns are stitched, sew them together in order. Once again, pay attention to the direction of the flying geese blocks.

FINISHING
THE QUILT

1. Cut and piece the backing fabric to create a backing that is at least 4" to 6" larger than the quilt top measurements.

2. Prepare the quilt sandwich and machine- or hand-quilt as desired (see page 153).

3. Bind the quilt as on page 155.

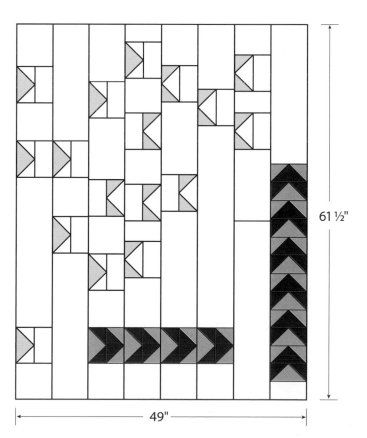

Rail
Fence

Forever Fencin' Rail Fence
Maker: Shelly Pagliai,
Prairie Moon Quilts; Ca. 2009;
Photo by Angel Massie,
Happenstance Photography

Three Sisters Rail Fence
Maker: Top unknown and
Mary Schafer (Flushing, MI);
Ca. 1915 (top) and
Ca. 1980 (completed);
83" x 98"; Cotton with
polyester filling; Michigan
State University Museum
#1998:53.103

RAIL FENCE INSPIRATION

◻ Although a simple and basic pattern, the Rail Fence can make a very bold and graphic statement through the designer's choice of fabrics. It is a very traditional pattern (not unlike the Log Cabin) that has been used for centuries in Europe, the Middle East, and Asia in mosaics, tiles, and paintings, as well as textiles. These quilts were typically made from old clothes and leftover textiles, and mostly made for utilitarian purposes. This is why you may find older Rail Fence quilts from the second half of the 19th century and the beginning of the 20th century made in wool, corduroy, and other garment fabrics.

What is it that attracts us to these simplistic blocks? Possibly, it's the ability to manipulate the materials so easily because the pattern is so basic. Many of the vintage or antique Rail Fence quilts are so bold and contemporary in color and pattern that I am amazed time and again when I look at the date of the quilt. It seems that we haven't invented anything new here! We are, however, exploring and pushing the boundaries that exist in what we consider traditional quilting (i.e. quilting that has been done over the past 50 years). Looking back at the work of those who designed before us will provide inspiration to us all.

◼ Marie Bostwick's traditional palette of bold colors along with her mitered borders create a more formal and historical feel. Heather Jones's very contemporary colors appear to be a more subtle choice in many ways; yet the boldness of the quilt comes from the large asymmetrical sizes of the strips that make up the blocks.

TRADITIONAL
RAIL FENCE

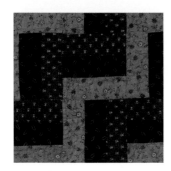

Rail Fence Lap Quilt

DESIGNED, PIECED AND QUILTED BY MARIE BOSTWICK

FINISHED DIMENSIONS Approximately 56" wide x 65" long

FABRIC

The fabric used for the quilt shown is from Jo Morton's "Savannah" collection by Andover Fabrics, Inc. Yardages are based on 44"/45"-wide fabric. Adjust yardage for different widths, as needed.

Fabric A (red print): 1 yard

Fabric B (black print): 1 yard

Fabric C (gold print): 1 yard

Fabric D (plain black): ¼ yard for border

Fabric E (striped print): 1½ yard for border (Includes 1 yard for bias binding)

Fabric F (floral print): ¾ yard for border

Backing fabric: 3½ yards

Batting: Twin size

INSPIRATION

The palette for my quilts is normally bright and bold. So when I was asked to create a traditional Rail Fence design, I wasn't quite sure I'd find fabrics that spoke to me. However, the minute I came across Jo Morton's "Savannah" collection, I knew we were in business. Though the colors in these fabrics are more saturated than those I would normally choose, the addition of a wide rail of black fabric adds richness. It makes a strong statement while respecting the traditional nature of this classic, time-honored pattern.

SUPPLIES

■ General Sewing Supplies (page 150)

■ MARIE BOSTWICK

Marie Bostwick is a *New York Times* and *USA Today* best-selling author of uplifting contemporary and historical fiction. Her *Cobbled Court Quilts* series of novels have gained an especially strong following among quilters. Marie's fifth novel, *Ties That Bind*, was named Best Mainstream Novel of 2012 by *RT BookReviews* magazine. Her 2013 release, *Between Heaven and Texas*, has been nominated for the same award. In the three decades since her marriage, she has lived in eight different states at eighteen different addresses. These experiences have given Marie a unique perspective that lets her write about people from all corners of the country with insight and authenticity. Aside from writing, Marie's great passion is quilting, which she took up 25 years ago, searching for a creative outlet while raising three wild boys. Though Marie considers herself a hobby quilter, her designs have appeared in national quilt magazines and she has been proud to serve a three-year term on the board of the Quilt Alliance. Currently, Marie lives in Connecticut and travels extensively to speak at bookstores, libraries, quilt guilds, and quilt shows throughout the country.

CUTTING THE FABRIC

Cut the following strips:

- Fabric A - 15 2" x width of fabric strips
- Fabric B - 15 2" x width of fabric strips
- Fabric C - 15 2" x width of fabric strips
- Fabric D - seven 1" x width of fabric strips for the first border
- Fabric E - seven 2½" x width of fabric strips for the second border
- Fabric F - seven 3½" x width of fabric strips for the third border

SEWING INSTRUCTIONS

All seams are sewn right sides together using a ¼" seam allowance unless otherwise indicated.

Assembling the Blocks

1. Stitch the 15 Fabric A strips to the fifteen Fabric B strips along one long edge. Press seam allowances toward Fabric A.

2. Stitch the 15 Fabric C strips to the long unstitched edge of the Fabric B strips. Press seam allowances toward Fabric B.

3. You now have 15 sewn three-strip units measuring 5" across. From each unit, cut eight 5" squares. You'll have 120 5" squares total.

4. Following the pattern in the diagram, sew four 5" squares together to make a larger, 9½" block. Repeat until you have 30 completed blocks.

Sewing the Center Section

1. Sew five of the larger 9½" blocks together (all facing the same direction) into a row measuring 45½" long. Repeat this step five more times, until you have six rows. Press the seam allowances of half the rows to the left. Press the allowances of the remaining rows to the right.

2. Making sure that the rows create the Rail Fence pattern across the entire quilt, sew the rows right sides together and matching the seams. This will complete the center section of your quilt, five blocks across and six blocks in length, to measure 45½" wide x 54½" long.

Adding the Borders

1. Sew the short ends of the border strips of fabric D, E, and F together to make two 58" strips and two 67" strips of each of the three border fabrics. The border strips are cut longer than the quilt size to allow for mitered corners.

2. Sew all three border strips (D, E and F) in each length together along the long edge. You will have two borders measuring 6" wide by 58" long for the top and bottom and two borders measuring 6" wide by 67" long for the two sides.

3. Sew the borders on all four sides of the quilt center, starting and stopping sewing ¼" away from the edge of the quilt. Miter the four corners, making sure to match the seams of the three border strips. Press well.

4. The finished quilt top should measure 56½" x 65½".

FINISHING THE QUILT

1. Cut and piece the backing fabric to create a backing that is at least 4" to 6" larger than the quilt-top measurements.

2. See page 153 for basting and quilting instructions. Quilt as desired.

3. Bind your quilt using your preferred method or refer to page 155 for binding directions.

MODERN
RAIL FENCE

Modern Rail Fence

INSPIRATION

This quilt is a modern interpretation of the traditional Rail Fence pattern. A quilt made by Plummer T. Pettway of Gee's Bend was my inspiration. I varied the widths of the rails throughout the layout to make it my own.

DESIGNED, PIECED, AND QUILTED BY HEATHER JONES

FINISHED DIMENSIONS Approximately 60" wide x 70" long

FABRIC

All fabrics are from FreeSpirit Designer Solids. Yardages are based on 44"/45"-wide fabric.

Fabric #1 Natural: 1½ yards

Fabric #2 Dogwood: 2 yards (includes ½ yard for binding)

Fabric #3 Cosmic Blue: 2¼ yards

Backing: 4½ yards

Batting: Twin size

SUPPLIES

- General Sewing Supplies (page 150)
- Blue painters tape or masking tape for labeling
- Sharpie marker

CUTTING THE FABRIC

There are a lot of different sized pieces of fabric. Mark their sizes with tape and a marker. Arrange them in stacks according to their widths (2½", 4½", or 6½") and keep note of the lengths during construction.

1. Fabric 1 Natural, cut:

- Two 2½" x width of fabric strips
  Sub-cut: Two 2½" x 10½" strips
  Two 2½" x 16½" strips

- Six 4½" x width of fabric strips
  Sub-cut: Six 4 ½" x 10½" strips
  Four 4½" x 16½" strips
  Four 4½" x 18½" strips

- Two 6½" x width of fabric strips
  Sub-cut: Three 6½" x 16½" strips

HEATHER JONES

Heather Jones is a designer and self-taught quilter who lives outside of Cincinnati with her husband and two young children. She is inspired by everyday places and things that many people wouldn't even notice (think an old metal silo or a painted grid in a parking lot). Heather has a great love and respect for the traditional art of quilting, is an avid collector of vintage quilts, and loves to bring a modern twist to traditional patterns. Her modern quilting patterns are available at a number of online locations and she will soon bring the Heather Jones Studio Patterns to print as well. Heather is currently working on her first solo publication for fall 2015.

2. Fabric 2 Dogwood, cut:

- One 2½" x width of fabric strip
  Sub-cut: One 2½" x 14½" strip
- Five 4½" x Width of fabric strips
  Sub-cut: Two 4½" x 8½" strips
  Three 4½" x 10½" strips
  Two 4½" x 16½" strips
  One 4½" x 18½" strip
  Two 4½" x 22½" strips
- Three 6½" x width of fabric strips
  Sub-cut: One 6½" x 10½" strip
  Two 6½" x 12½" strips
  Two 6½" x 14½" strips
  Two 6½" x 16½" strips

3. Fabric 3 Cosmic Blue, cut:

- Two 2½" x width of fabric strips
  Sub-cut: Two 2½" x 10½" strips
  Two 2½" x 16½" strips
  One 2½" x 18½" strip
- Seven 4½" x width of fabric strips
  Sub-cut: Two 4½" x 8½" strips
  Four 4½" x 10½" strips
  Two 4½" x 14½" strips
  Six 4½" x 16½" strips
  One 4½" x 18½" strip
  One 4½" x 22½" strip

- Five 6½" x width of fabric strips
  Sub-cut: One 6½" x 10½" strip
  One 6½" x 12½" strip
  One 6½" x 14½" strip
  Three 6½" x 16½" strips
  Two 6½" x 18½" strips
  One 6½" x 22½" strip

SEWING INSTRUCTIONS

Sew all pieces right sides together with a ¼" seam. Press seam allowances to one side, toward the darker fabric.

Assembling the Quilt Top

The quilt top is constructed in four columns, lettered A to D, each consisting of five blocks numbered 1 to 5. Follow the diagram for placement of the strip pieces using the size of the strips indicated from your stacks.

1. Sew the following blocks together to construct column A:

- Block A1 – 10½" x 20½":
  Three 4½" x 10½" Fabric 1
  and two 4½" x 10½" Fabric 3
- Block A2 – 10½" x 10½":
  Two 4½" x 10½" Fabric 2
  and one 2½" x 10½" Fabric 3.
- Block A3 – 10½"" x 6 ½":
  Two 2½" x 10½" Fabric 1
  and one 2½" x 10½" Fabric 3
- Block A4 – 10½" x 14½":
  One 2½" x 14½" Fabric 2
  and two 4½" x 14½" Fabric 3
- Block A5 – 10½" x 20½":
  Three 4½" x 10½" Fabric 1
  and two 4½" x 10½" Fabric 3

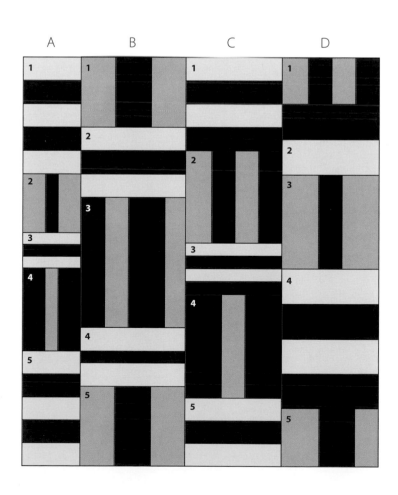

2. Sew the following blocks together to construct column B:

- Block B1 – 18½" x 12½": Two 6½" x 12½" Fabric 2 and one 6½" x 12½" Fabric 3
- Block B2 – 18½" x 12½": Two 4½" x 18½" Fabric 1 and one 4½" x 18½" Fabric 3
- Block B3 – 18½" x 22 ½": Two 4½" x 22½" Fabric 2, one 4½" x 22½" Fabric 3 and one 6 ½" x 22 ½" Fabric 3
- Block B4 – 18½" x 10½": Two 4½" x 18½" Fabric 1 and one 2½" x 18½" Fabric 3
- Block B5 – 18½" x 14½": Two 6½" x 14½" Fabric 2 and one 6½" x 14½" Fabric 3

3. Sew the following blocks together to construct column C:

- Block C1 – 16½" x 16½": Two 4½" x 16½" Fabric 1 and two 4½" x 16½" Fabric 3
- Block C2 – 16½" x 16½": Two 4½" x 16½" Fabric 2 and two 4½" x 16½" Fabric 3
- Block C3 – 16½" x 8½": Two 2½" x 16½" Fabric 1 and two 2½" x 16½" Fabric 3
- Block C4 – 16½" x 18½": One 4½" x 18½" Fabric 2 and two 6½" x 18½" Fabric 3
- Block C5 - 16½" x 12½": Two 4½" x 16½" Fabric 1 and one 4½" x 16½" Fabric 3

4. Sew the following blocks together to construct column D:

- Block D1 – 16½" x 8½": Two 4½" x 8½" Fabric 2 and two 4½" x 8½" Fabric 3
- Block D2 – 16½" x 12½": One 6½" x 16½" Fabric 1 and one 6½" x 16½" Fabric 3
- Block D3 – 16½" x 16½": Two 6½" x 16½" Fabric 2 and one 4½" x 16½" Fabric 3
- Block D4 – 16½" x 24½": Two 6½" x 16½" Fabric 1 and two 6½" x 16½" Fabric 3
- Block D5 – 16½" x 10½": One 4½" x 10½" Fabric 2, one 6½" x 10½" Fabric 2 and one 6½" x 10½" Fabric 3

5. Following the diagram, sew columns A, B, C, and D together to finish the quilt top.

FINISHING THE QUILT

1. Create the quilt back. Cut two 68" x width of fabric pieces from the backing fabric. Remove the selvages and sew the two pieces right sides together, along the long edge of the fabric. Press seam allowances to one side.

2. Layer the quilt top, batting, and quilt back to make a quilt sandwich (see page 153). Baste together with pins or basting stitches.

3. Quilt as desired. Trim off any excess batting and fabric after quilting, and square up all sides.

4. Cut seven 2½" x width of fabric strips from the binding fabric. Cut off the selvages and sew the seven strips together to create the binding. Bind the quilt as desired (see page 158).

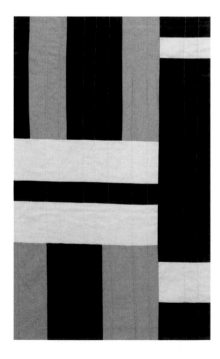

Templates

Photocopy the appropriate template or templates as instructed (at 100% unless otherwise noted). Cut them out by hand, and transfer to cardstock if desired. Then use as described in the instructions provided for the quilt.

PERMISSION TO PHOTOCOPY

DOUBLE WEDDING RING

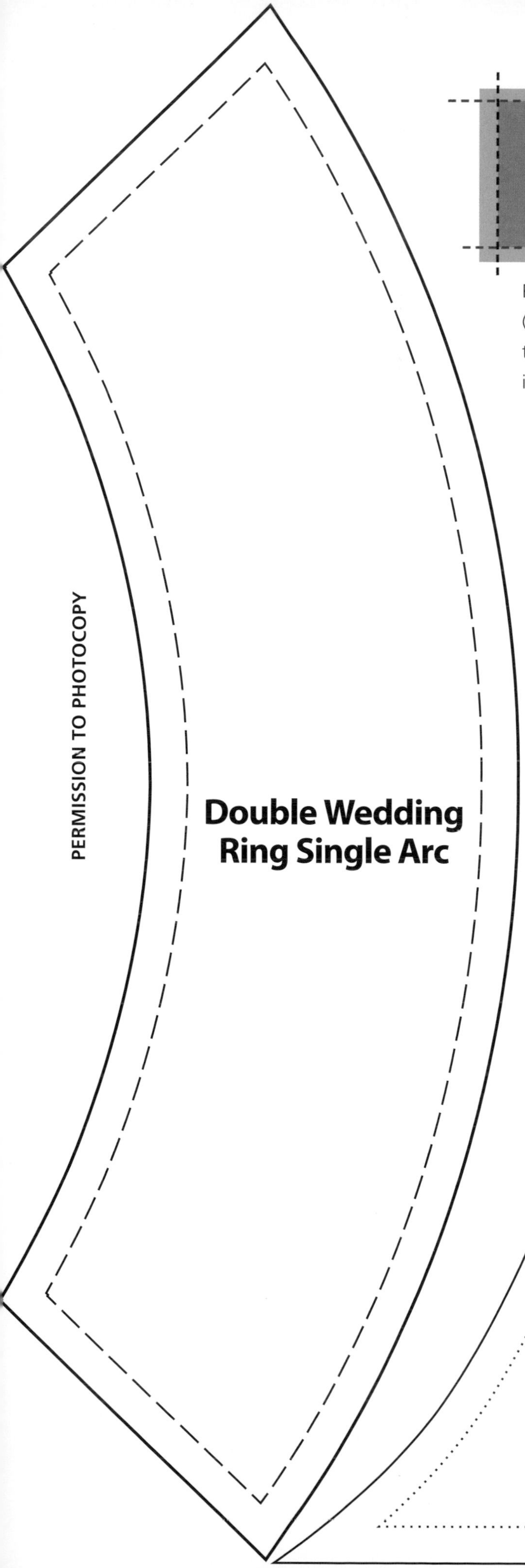
Double Wedding Ring Single Arc

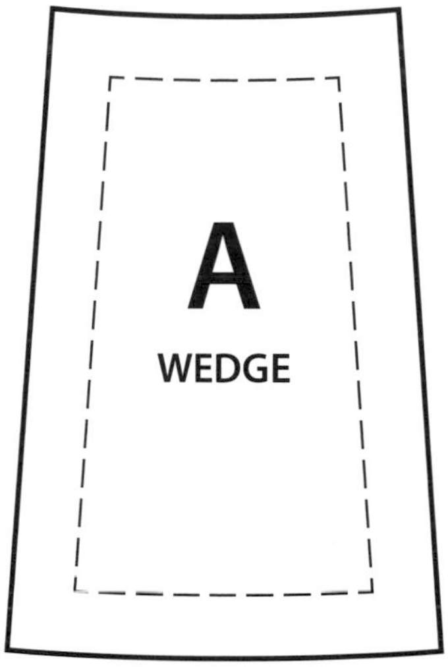
A
WEDGE

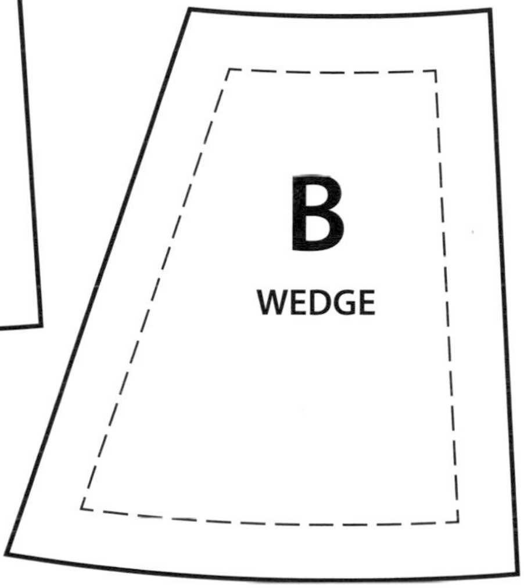
B
WEDGE

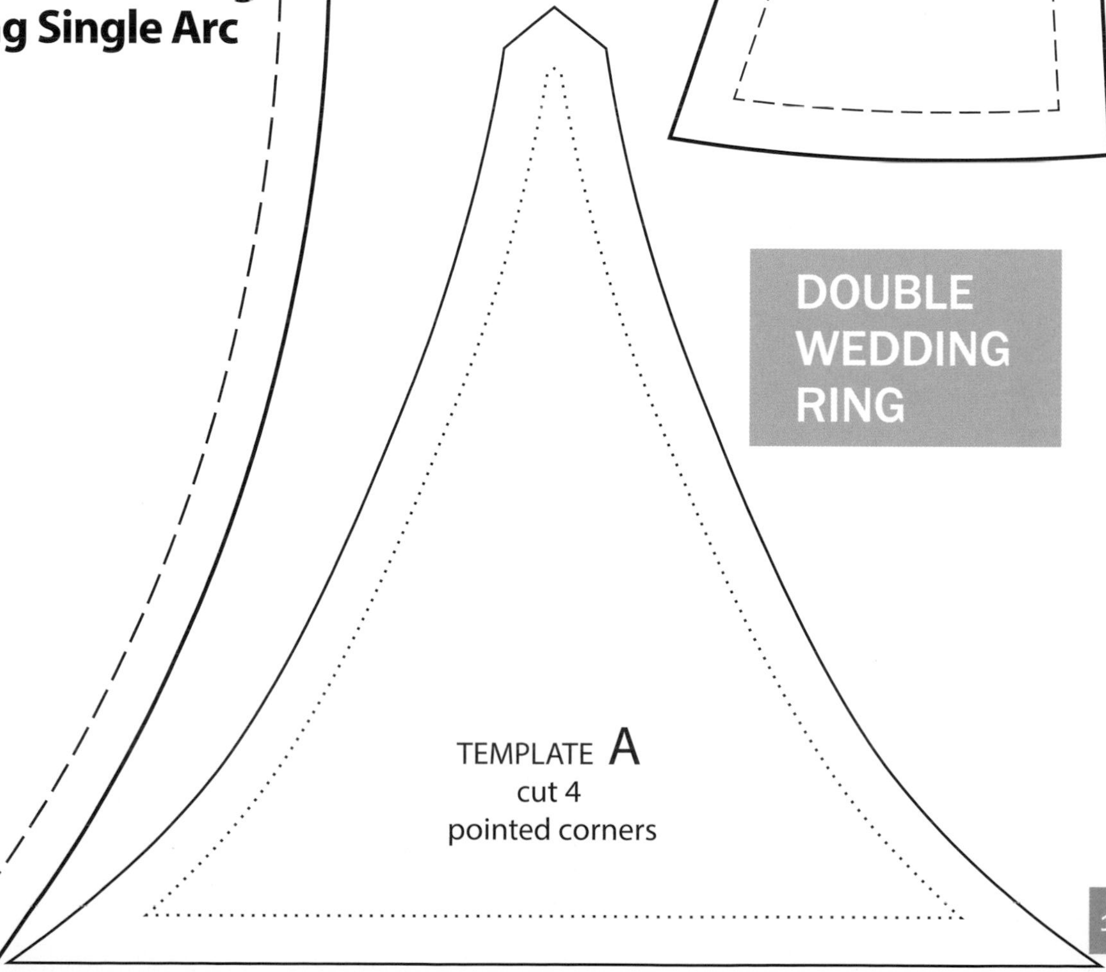
TEMPLATE A
cut 4
pointed corners

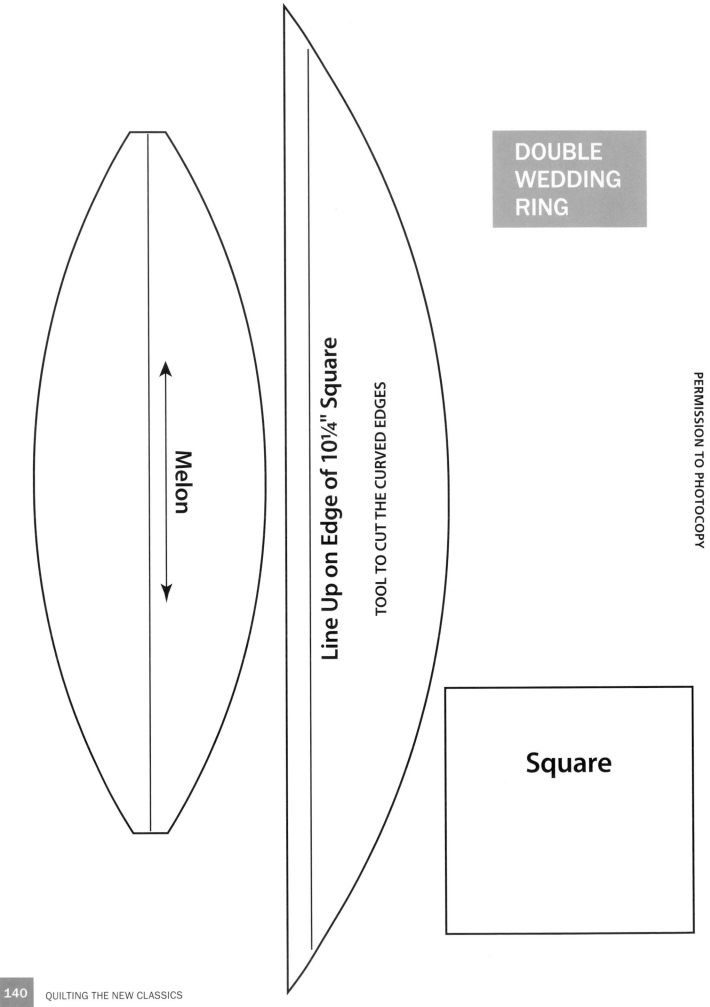

Melon

Line Up on Edge of 10¼" Square

TOOL TO CUT THE CURVED EDGES

DOUBLE WEDDING RING

Square

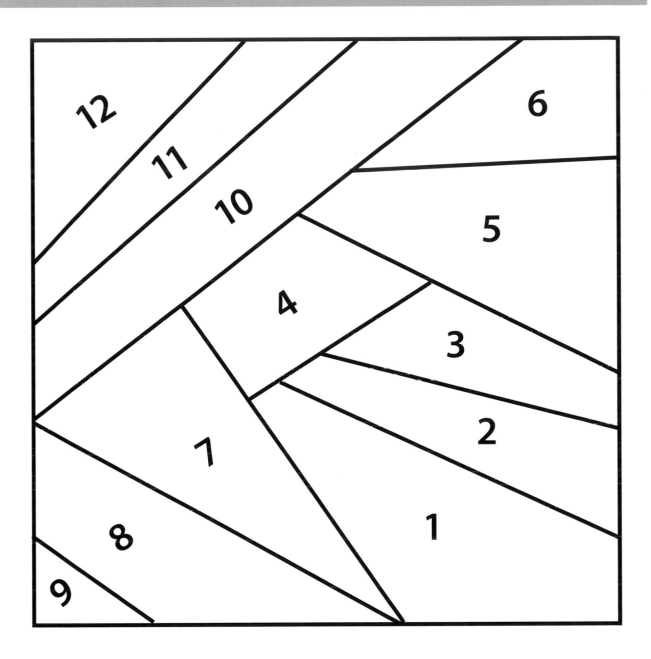

PERMISSION TO PHOTOCOPY

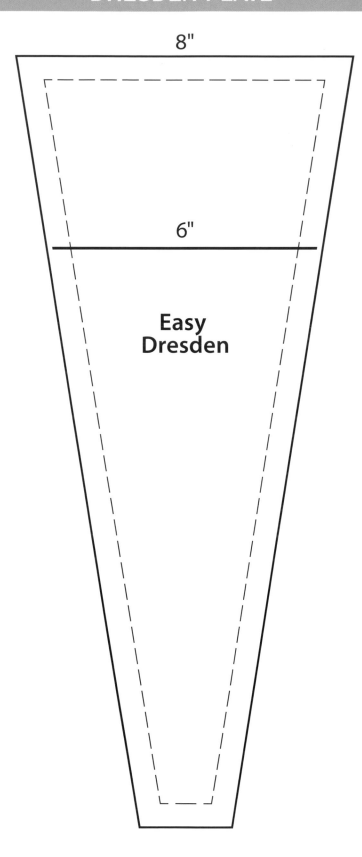

8"

6"

Easy Dresden

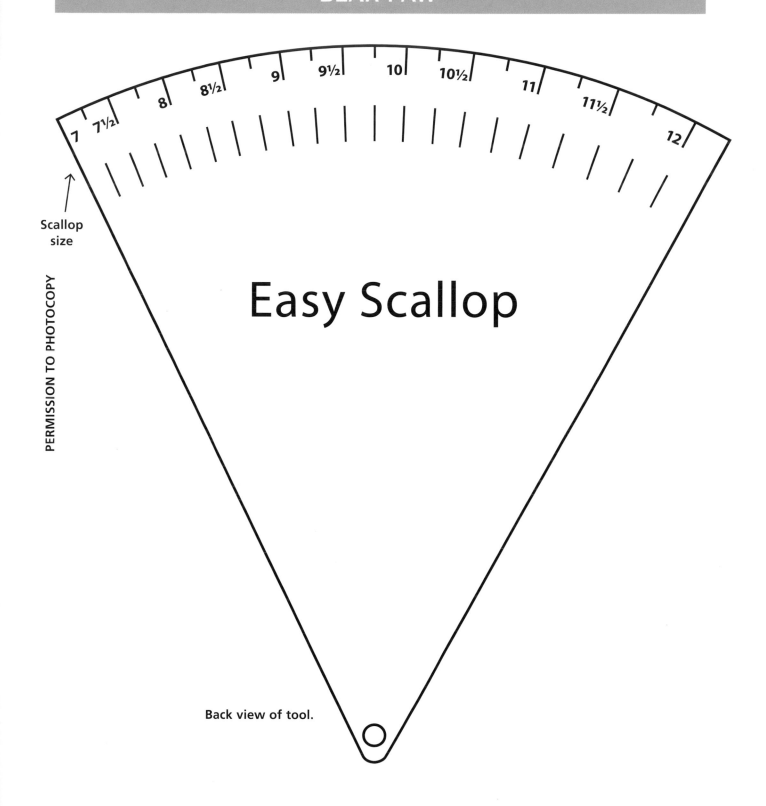

Scallop
size

PERMISSION TO PHOTOCOPY

Easy Scallop

Back view of tool.

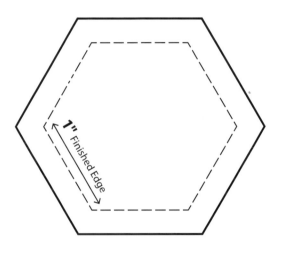

1"
Finished Edge

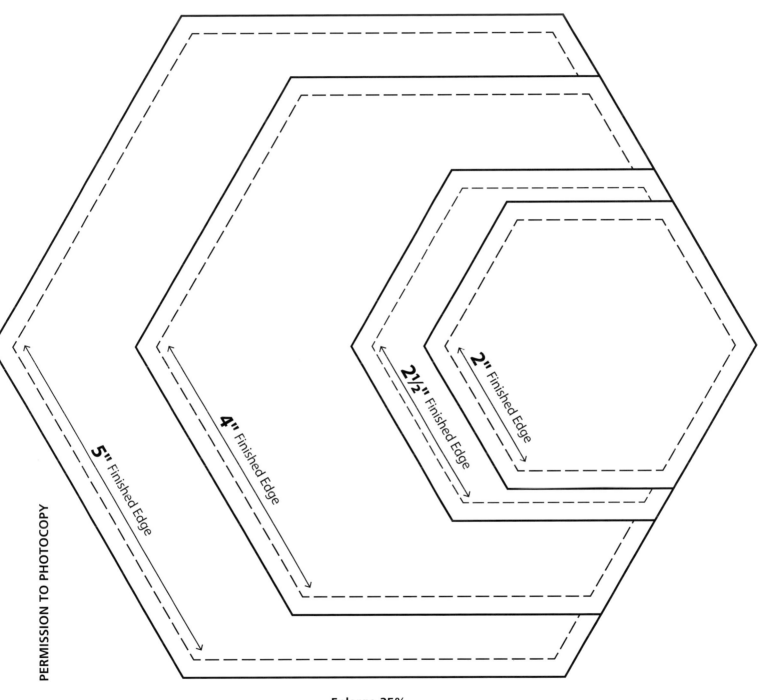

PERMISSION TO PHOTOCOPY

5" Finished Edge

4" Finished Edge

2½" Finished Edge

2" Finished Edge

Enlarge 35%.

YO-YO

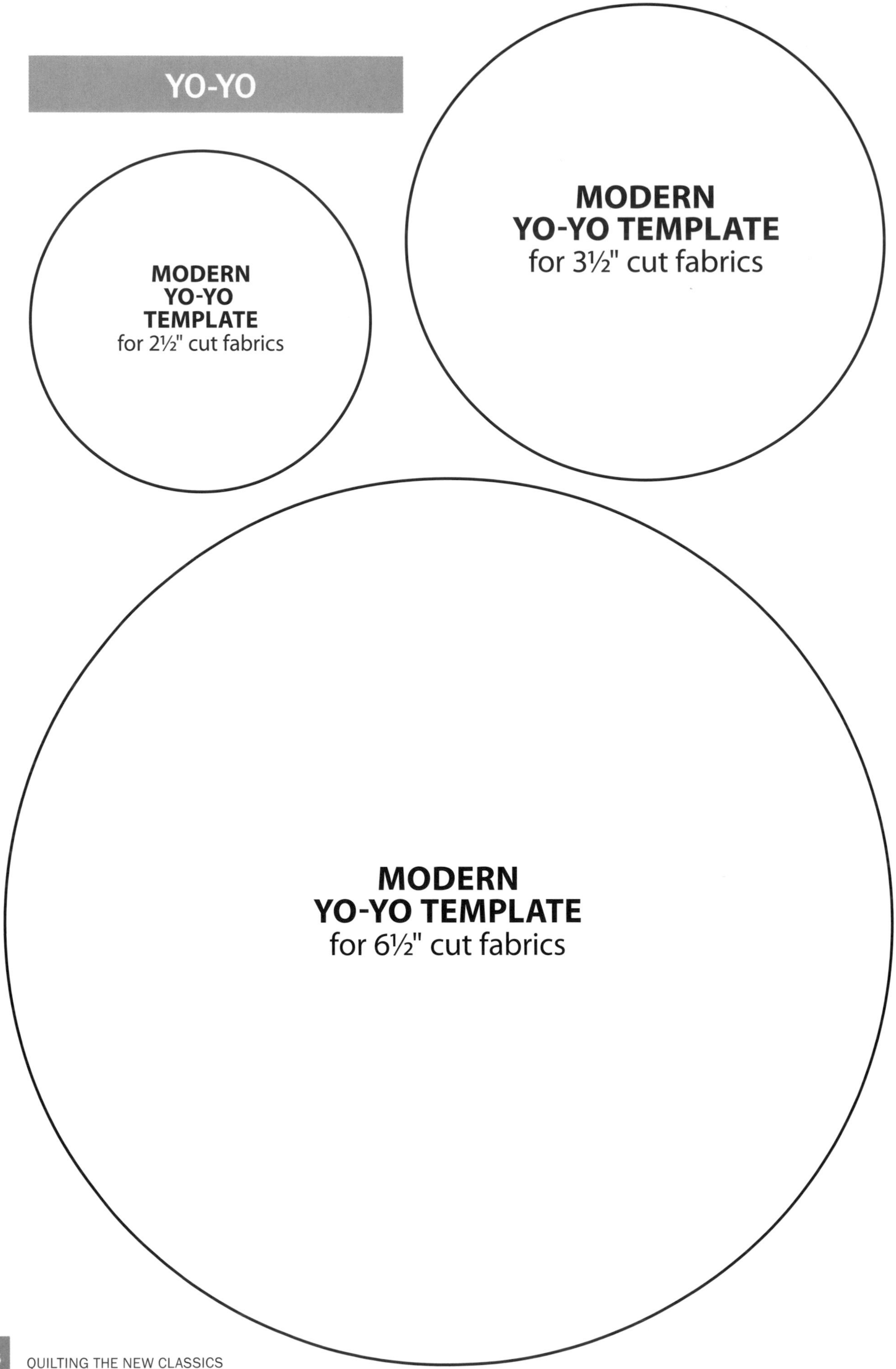
MODERN YO-YO TEMPLATE
for 3½" cut fabrics
MODERN YO-YO TEMPLATE
for 2½" cut fabrics
MODERN YO-YO TEMPLATE
for 6½" cut fabrics

PERMISSION TO PHOTOCOPY

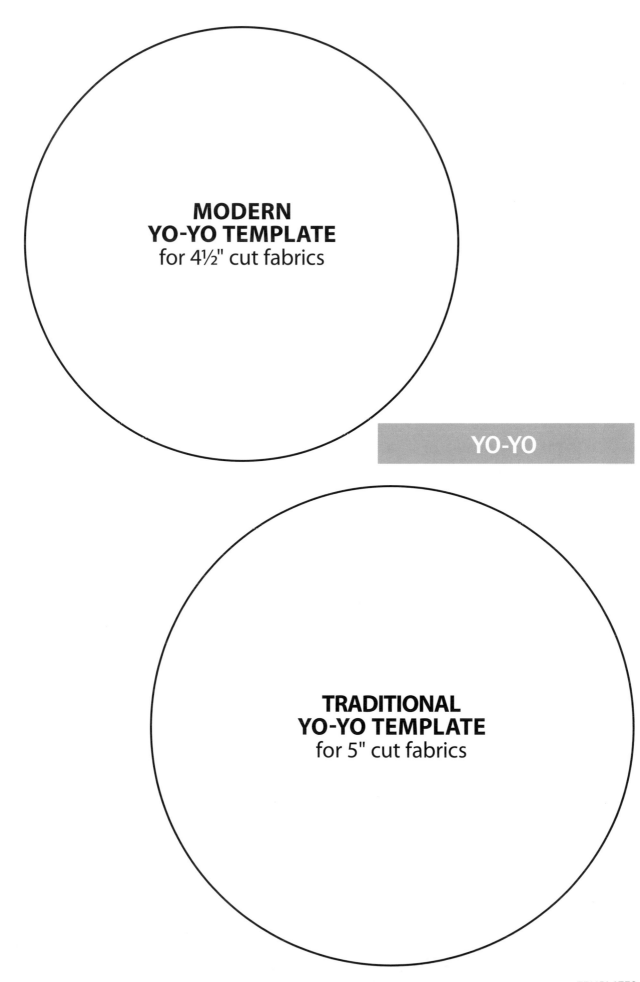

**MODERN
YO-YO TEMPLATE**
for 4½" cut fabrics

YO-YO

**TRADITIONAL
YO-YO TEMPLATE**
for 5" cut fabrics

Essential
Techniques

BASIC TOOLS, SUPPLIES &
QUILTING KNOW-HOW

Getting Started

GENERAL SEWING SUPPLIES

The following basic tools and supplies are all you truly need to create the featured quilts.

- Sewing machine
- Iron and ironing board
- Machine- and hand-sewing needles
- Fabric shears
- Sewing scissors
- Rotary cutter and mat

- Rotary cutting rulers (12" square and 6½" x 24" rectangle)
- Coordinating threads
- Decorative threads (optional)
- Temporary fabric marking tools* (water, heat, or air-soluble)
- Straight pins

- Nickel-plated brass safety pins, size 1 or 2 for basting
- Binding clips

Be sure to test any fabric marking tool on scrap fabric before marking your quilt.

FABRIC CHOICES

CONTRIBUTED BY TERESA COATES, ROBERT KAUFMAN FABRICS

First hand-stitched from scraps of linens and silks taken from old clothing, quilts have been made for hundreds of years. Over the centuries, quilting has evolved and yet, in many ways, stayed the same. Whole cloth, patchwork, appliqué, crazy quilting, and medallion quilts are all historical and yet contemporary.

As quilting resurged in popularity over the past decade, fabric choices have multiplied and quilters are repeating history with a fascination for linen, as well as looking to new substrates to add texture, dimension, and a dash of intrigue to their quilting. Pure 100% cotton remains a favorite for many quilters because it is so easy to sew.

Today's quilters use to their advantage the wide array of fabrics available. Each fabric listed below offers a unique look and feel to a quilt, appealing to quilters in different ways.

Quilting Cotton

In a wide variety of prints and solids, cotton has long been a favorite among quilters. Its predisposition to shrinking gives a soft look and elicits a nostalgic feeling. It is often sold in "fat quarters," which are cut specifically to suit the needs of quilters. Cottons are also sold in coordinated collections, making it easy to mix and match prints and/or solids.

Linen

Probably the first fabric used to create quilts, it is regaining popularity. Linen adds texture and depth to designs, but care should be taken, as the raw edges are prone to fraying. Shorten your stitch length to prevent puckering. You might also consider using cotton/linen blends for the best of both fabrics.

Denim

Offered in a variety of weights, denim is typically used for patchwork and backing. Denim can add both weight and longevity to a quilt. Washed and treated denims are perfect for contemporary design interest.

Chambray

Known for its soft hand, chambray is heavier than quilting cotton and lends a casual feel to patchwork quilts.

Corduroy

Narrow-wale corduroy has a soft velvet-like feel, adding texture and warmth to a quilt. Pre-wash the yardage to diminish the lint build-up when quilting. You might also want to stitch along the raw edges to prevent raveling.

Batik

Tightly woven and reversible, batiks are traditionally made with wax reliefs and lend an exotic feel to all types of quilts. It is a favorite for art quilting because of its array of colors and because it doesn't fray.

Flannel

A favorite for baby quilts, flannels have a soft hand and are gentle to the touch.

BATTING

COMPILED BY MICHELE MUSKA

When it came to finding the best batting for my first bed quilt, I was completely stumped, so I went to an expert, Judy Novella from Fairfield Processing (www.fairfieldworld.com).

I was surprised when she had so many questions for me. What kind of drape do you want? Do you want it for warmth? What type of loft? And how are you going to quilt it? So, I asked if she could help us all out by outlining some of the most important aspects of quilt batting.

For many quilters, the batting aisle can be a confusing wall of white. Take into consideration the following factors: fiber content, quilting method, desired effect, end use, and care requirements. In most cases, several battings will work great for a particular quilt and ultimately you will decide which battings are best for you.

Fiber Content

Natural and renewable fibers, such as cotton and wool, are commonly used and typically preferred over synthetic fibers for their natural origins and breathability. They will shrink with the first washing and get softer with use.

Cotton battings are flat (low-loft) and are easy to use because fabric clings to the cotton batting, making it easy to baste without shifting. In larger sizes, cotton batting can be heavy. It will have a very flat drape, making it suitable for wall hangings and table décor projects.

Wool batting is very warm with a medium loft that provides nice stitch definition. It is lighter than cotton with a softer drape and is preferred by many art quilters. It is also crease-resistant; a desirable trait if a quilt will be folded for a period of time.

Bamboo-rayon batting is made from the cellulose of abundant bamboo grass and has a silky quality. It is gaining in popularity because it is light, crease-resistant, and decadently soft.

Polyester batting is the most popular synthetic fiber because it is lightweight and has a soft drape that allows the quilt to wrap around you comfortably. It is available in a tremendous variety of lofts, offers insulating warmth, doesn't shrink, and releases creases. By nature, it will withstand years of use and abuse, without altering its original loft or wearing out.

DON'T FORGET BLENDS

They are engineered to perform in a specific way by marrying individual characteristics of the component fibers. The specific characteristics of each blend are determined by the fiber balance, fiber types, and manufacturing methods. For instance, a 70% cotton/ 30% polyester batting will have a weight and quilted effect like 100% cotton, yet will resist creases like polyester.

Cotton/bamboo/rayon batting has a silky texture that is supple and soft. It results in a light summer-weight quilt with a low loft. Quilts made with this type of batting will remain soft and supple even with dense machine quilting or heavy thread painting.

Quilting Method

Certain types of batting lend themselves to specific methods of quilting.

Hand Quilting is best done with scrim-free battings. Scrim is a polyester grid that stabilizes cotton batting. Battings with a scrim are harder to quilt by hand and can be eliminated from the batting choices.

Machine Quilting is the quickest method and can be done with any and all types of battings.

Tied Quilting is a quick method of securing quilt layers with knots, but it does create stress points in the batting. Battings that are needle punched and do not have a scrim should be avoided when using this method. You should refer to packaging for this information. Battings with scrim are the "strongest" and are recommended when a natural-fiber batting is preferred. Polyester battings that are bonded can be tied and offer more options when it comes to loft.

Desired Effect, End Use, and Care Requirements

How you want the quilt to look and its end use will factor into your batting-choice decision.

Loft is an indication of weight and thickness. Low-loft batting is thin and is often used for wall hangings and table décor. High-loft batting is typically used when warmth and a fluffier appearance is desired. For instance, if a very dimensional "trapunto" effect is desired, then the batting needs to have a medium or high loft, which is most common in polyester and wool battings. If a flat, vintage effect is desired, then the batting should be made with a natural fiber such as cotton. Wool batting is usually the thickest batting, while bamboo is the lightest and drapes beautifully.

Quilts used as bedding should be comfortable, with a soft drape. Quilts made with polyester batting are lightweight and provide insulating warmth. Bed quilts made with 100% cotton provide a weightier comfort that breathes. Cotton can be stiff if heavily quilted, yet tends to soften with repeated washings.

Washing is a consideration. Bedding quilts will require frequent washings. All battings can be washed by hand or machine, as appropriate for the quilt itself. Polyester batting will maintain its loft and will not shrink, regardless of how frequently it's laundered. Cotton battings shrink with the first washing and soften with multiple launderings.

> **TIP** *Preshrinking is not recommended by batting manufacturers because the batting doesn't have the integrity of fabric and may be compromised during the preshrinking process. Batting should be considered fragile until it is quilted between fabric layers (never agitate or wring unquilted batting). Any shrinking will be limited to the first washing and will enhance the effect of the finished quilt.*

Display options also influence batting choices. Art quilters tend to favor cotton, cotton blends, and wool battings for quilts that are designed to hang. These battings drape straighter and have a stiffer hand than polyester battings. Art quilts are not usually laundered, so care requirements are not as fundamental to choosing the batting.

Quilting Fundamentals

CONTRIBUTED BY BARBARA PARSONS CARTIER

Your beautiful quilt top is pieced and you love it! Now, how to quilt it? Would your design be best enhanced with an all-over quilt pattern? Or, would you like to highlight some of the design elements? Maybe the design speaks for itself and outline quilting is your best choice. Study your quilt top and listen to it. You will find that it will tell you what it wants.

PREPARING THE QUILT FOR QUILTING

- Before basting and quilting, check to be sure the quilt top is square and lays flat. Use a 6" x 24" quilting ruler or a T-square to check each corner inside the borders and along the outside edges. Make adjustments at this point to ensure the quilt will be fairly square after quilting.

- Consider attaching your quilt label to the backing before quilting so that the quilting stitches will make it a permanent part of the quilt.

- Press the top and the backing before basting.

- If the quilting design requires it, mark the quilt before basting with a marking tool that is easily washed out. Always test the marking tool on scraps first.

- The backing and batting should be 2 to 3 inches larger than the top on all sides to allow for shrinkage from quilting.

- Make the "quilt sandwich" and baste it on a hard flat surface. Spread the backing wrong side up and tape it down in several places with masking tape to prevent it from shifting during the basting process. Next lay the batting on top, gently smoothing it out from the center to the edges. Finally, place the quilt top on the batting, carefully centering it to the backing.

- Begin basting in the center of the quilt and progress out to the edges, smoothing as you go. Thread-basting with long running stitches is used when hand-quilting. Basting for machine-quilting is best done with size 1 or 2 nickel-plated brass safety pins, which do not rust and may remain in the quilt for some time. The curved basting safety pins are easy to use but are not a necessity. Pin the quilt every 4 to 6 inches; the more pins used, the better. They ensure that the layers do not shift during machine-quilting.

- Fold in the quilt edges and secure with safety pins to protect the batting during quilting.

QUILTING BASICS

Hand-quilting is done with a running stitch. The goal of course is tiny even stitches, but don't worry if your stitches aren't initially tiny. They will become smaller with practice. More important is the uniformity of the stitches: Strive to make them equal in size and evenly spaced.

Machine-quilting is faster than hand-quilting and can be accomplished on a home sewing machine or a long-arm machine. There are many resources that explain in great detail how to machine-quilt. Take the time to explore these resources and be patient. It takes practice to perfect this art.

Following are a few pointers for quilting on your home sewing machine.

- Place a large table next to the sewing machine to support the entire quilt while it is under the needle. Having the sewing machine bed at table level prevents drag on the quilt during sewing.

- Clean the bobbin area and feed dogs throughout quilting.

- A walking foot can be used for gentle curves as well as straight lines.

- Size 11 machine quilting needles work well. Titanium needles are a little more expensive but are worth it because they stay sharp for a very long time. Experiment with different kinds of needles to find out which ones work best with your thread and on your machine. Keep notes so you can remember what works best.

- There are so many threads to choose from that books are written on this subject alone. Cotton 50-weight thread is light-weight and blends into the quilt so it doesn't detract from the design. Heavier-weight thread or decorative thread can invigorate the quilt and add design elements. Have fun experimenting with the beautiful thread choices that are available. Again, take notes.

- Softly bunch up the quilt on the table, making a depression of the area to be quilted. Use both hands to guide the quilt under the needle and concentrate only on the area between your hands. It is very important that you do not remove your hands from the quilt while the machine is in motion. This cannot be stressed enough. Activate the "needle-down" option, if it is available, to keep the needle in place whenever you stop sewing.

- Keep a distant perspective. Focusing closely on the quilting can make all of the little inconsistencies in the stitches seem conspicuous and this can be distressing. Step away and look at the total quilt and all of those discrepancies melt away.

- Machine-quilting takes practice to master. Don't be too critical of yourself. Just do it! With time, you will find your rhythm.

- Remember to breathe and stretch. Periodically get up and away from the machine. Make yourself a cup of tea. Let your hands direct the quilt, not your mind. Listen to music or an audio book or television to keep your mind occupied and out of the way of the quilt.

After you are finished quilting, but before binding, check to be sure the quilt is still square and lays flat. If it got a little out of whack during the quilting process, carefully and gently pull on the excess backing and batting to ease it back to square.

If the quilt is to be hung, consider damp-blocking it to be sure it hangs straight and square. To block your quilt or quilt top, dampen with water using a spray bottle. Pin to a carpet or foam blocks, making sure it is the appropriate size. Allow to dry in place.

Quilt Binding

MAKING A BIAS BINDING STRIP

Bias binding is used to finish the edges of your quilt.

1. Take a rectangular piece of fabric cut on the straight (lengthwise) grain and fold the fabric diagonally at one end to find the true bias.

2. Using the bias fold as your guide, mark parallel lines on the fabric that are the width of your bias binding strip. Mark as many bias strips as needed to make your desired length binding strip, allowing for a ¼" seam allowance. (figure 1)

3. Cut away the triangular ends but do not cut along the marked lines. (figure 1)

4. On the marked fabric (step 2 above), join the shorter ends with right sides together. One strip will extend beyond the edge at each side. (figure 2)

5. Stitch a ¼" seam and press it open.

6. Begin cutting on the marked line at one end and continue cutting in a circular fashion. (figure 3)

PREPARING THE BIAS BINDING STRIP

1. Cut and stitch your binding strips per the instructions for your project, then press the seams flat.

2. With wrong sides together, fold the strip in half lengthwise and press lightly. Open the strip, lay it wrong side up, and fold each raw edge in toward the pressed center fold; press. (figure 4)

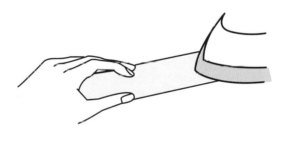

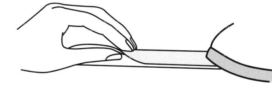

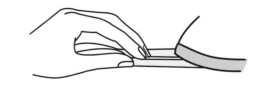

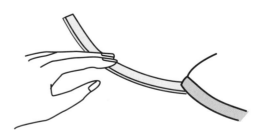

Figure 4

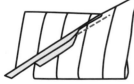

Figure 1

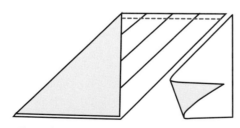

Figure 2   Figure 3

APPLYING THE BIAS BINDING STRIP

There are two ways to apply binding:
the single-fold method or double-fold method.

Single-fold Method

This type of binding is neat and flat. It is a good choice if you are working with bulkier fabric.

1. Lay your binding strip around all the edges it will cover. Adjust its placement to avoid placing the binding's seams at the corners where they'll add too much bulk. Leave at least 1" of the binding strip free at the beginning and end of the application for finishing.

2. Open the binding strip and with right sides together and all raw edges aligned, pin it to the right side of the edge being bound, beginning in the middle of one long edge.
NOTE: If the binding will go around corners, see "Mitering Binding Corners" (on page 157) before moving to the next step.

3. Baste the strip with a seam allowance ⅛" less than the width of the finished binding, then stitch the seam next to, but not on, the basting. Pull the basting threads to remove them. (figure 5)

4. Turn the bias strip over the seam allowance. Pin in place and slipstitch the folded edge of the strip to the item. (figure 6)

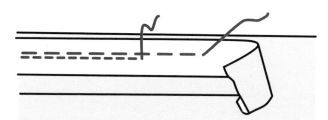

Figure 5

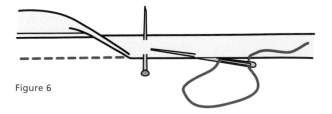

Figure 6

Double-fold Quilt-binding Method

This type of binding makes for stronger, long-lasting edges.

1. Fold the joined strip in half lengthwise with wrong sides together; press.

2. With the quilt top facing up and with raw edges aligned, pin the strip around the perimeter of the quilt. Baste in place ⅜" from the raw edges. (figure 7)

3. Stitch the binding strip to the quilt using a ½" seam allowance, mitering the corners. (figure 7)
To miter the corners, follow steps 2 to 5 of "Mitering Binding Corners" on page 157.

4. Turn the strip over the seam allowance to the quilt backing and slipstitch in place. (figure 8)

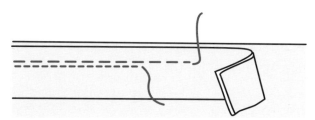

Figure 7

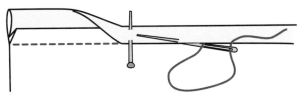

Figure 8

MITERING BINDING CORNERS

Bindings can bunch up in corners, so when you're binding a quilt, you'll need to miter the strip at the corners to get rid of excess fabric.

1. Open out one pre-folded edge of the binding strip and pin it in place.

2. Stitch to the corner and backstitch for reinforcement. (figure 9)

3. Fold the strip diagonally, as shown, to bring it around the corner. Pin, then stitch the adjoining edge through the corner from one end to the other end. (figure 10)

4. Fold the binding to form a miter on the right side and turn the bias strip over the seam allowance. (figure 11)

5. To finish the mitered corner on the wrong side, form a miter (with the fold of the miter in the opposite direction from the one formed on the right side to evenly distributed the bulk of the miter). (figure 12)

6. Turn, pin, and slipstitch the binding over the seamline, fastening the miter at the corner. (figure 12)

> **TIP** *Quick Finish For Binding Strips*
>
> *Apply the binding up to the point where it will be finished, leaving about 1" of extra binding strip. Trim the excess binding to between ¼" and ⅜" and then fold the raw ends of the binding under, inside the strip. Press, then slipstitch in place.*

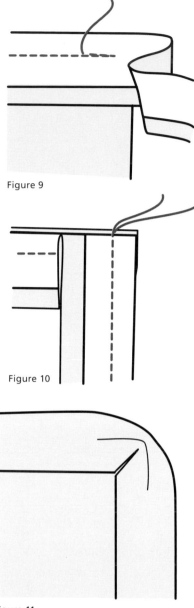

Figure 9

Figure 10

Figure 11

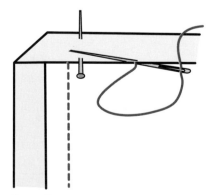

Figure 12

SUGGESTED READING

Aller, Allie.
Allie Aller's Crazy Quilting.
Lafayette: C&T Publishing, Inc.,
2011.

Brackman, Barbara.
*Encyclopedia of Pieced
Quilt Patterns.*
Paducah: American Quilter's
Society, 1993.

**Duke, Dennis and Harding,
Deborah (ed.).**
America's Glorious Quilt.
Beaux Arts Editions, 1987.

Findlay Wolfe, Victoria.
15 Minutes of Play. Lafayette:
C&T Publishing, Inc., 2012.

**Gering, Jacquie and
Pedersen, Katie.**
Quilting Modern. New York:
Interweave Press LLC, 2012.

Kiracofe, Roderick with text
from Mary Elizabeth Johnson.
*The American Quilt, A History of
Cloth and Comfort 1750-1950.*
New York: Clarkson Potter, 1993.

*Minnesota Quilts, Creating
Connections With Our Past.*
Text by Minnesota Quilt Project,
St. Paul: Voyager Press, 2005.

Orlofsky, Patsy and Myron.
Quilts in America. New York:
Abbeville Press, 1992.

Shaw, Robert.
*American Quilts, The Democratic
Art, 1780 – 2007.* New York:
Sterling Publishing Co., 2009.

Smucker, Janneken.
*Amish Quilts, Crafting an
American Icon.* Baltimore:
The Johns Hopkins University Press,
2013.

Waldvogel, Merikay.
Soft Cover for Hard Times.
Nashville: Rutledge Hill Press, 1990.

RESOURCES

www.accuquilt.com
for die cutting machine
and templates

www.allianceforamericanquilts.org
The Quilt Alliance

www.artemisinc.com
for Hannah Silk™

www.BarbaraParsonsCartier.com
for tech editing services

www.cherrywoodfabrics.com
for hand-dyed fabrics

www.cvquiltworks.com
Canton Village Quilt Works

www.delectablemountain.com
for natural fiber cloth

www.fairfieldworld.com
for quilt batting

www.lolare.com
for design and lifestyle inspiration

www.museum.msu.edu
Michigan State University Museum

www.nequiltmuseum.org
New England Quilt Museum

www.quiltindex.org
The Quilt Index

www.quiltstudy.org
International Quilt Study Center
and Museum

www.robertkaufman.com
for quilting and apparel fabric

www.sjquiltmuseum.org
San Jose Museum of Quilts
and Textiles

www.simplicity.com
for EZ Quilting notions
and templates

PHOTO CREDITS

Michele Muska's image on the back flap, courtesy of WWCreate

BIBLIOGRAPHY

Aller, Allie. *Allie Aller's Crazy Quilting.* Lafayette: C&T Publishing, Inc., 2011.

Brackman, Barbara. *Encyclopedia of Pieced Quilt Patterns.* Paducah: American Quilter's Society, 1993.

Kiracofe, Roderick, with text from Mary Elizabeth Johnson. *The American Quilt, A History of Cloth and Comfort 1750-1950.* New York: Clarkson Potter, 1993.

Shaw, Robert. American Quilts, *The Democratic Art, 1780 – 2007.* New York: Sterling Publishing Co., 2009.

SPECIAL CONTRIBUTORS

Labeling: Leslie Tucker Jennison
Fabric: Teresa Coates, Robert Kaufman Fabrics
Batting: Judy Novella, Fairfield Processing
Quilting and Technical Editor: Barbara Parsons Cartier
Museums: San Jose Museum of Quilts and Textiles, Michigan State University Museum, and The New England Quilt Museum

San Jose Museum of Quilts and Textiles:

The mission of the San Jose Museum of Quilts and Textiles is to promote and celebrate the art, creators, craft, and history of quilts and textiles. Just as founders created the museum through vision and heroic volunteer efforts, current and new generations of volunteers, artists, quilters, crafters and patrons partner with staff and board members to imagine and ensure the museum's present and future. The museum is the nexus for fiber artists, art lovers, collectors, quilters, and crafters who share a passion for fiber art and a deep commitment to its preservation and evolution.

Importance of Quilt Labels

A quilt label adds value to a quilt. It tells a story that strengthens the artistry of the piece. A label can offer the maker's name, date of completion, and the city where the quilt was constructed. It can also note a special occasion, such as a wedding, birth, or anniversary. Or more. Every piece of information included by the quilt artist has special meaning— both for the original recipient, as well as everyone who encounters the quilt in the future.

Michigan State University Museum:

Michigan State University Museum hosts the Great Lakes Quilt Center, which is dedicated to researching, documenting, preserving, and presenting quilt history. The center is an affiliate of the Center for Great Lakes Culture and a Regional Center for the Quilt/The Alliance for American Quilts. The museum holds one of the world's most significant quilt collections because of the diversity of its holdings, its rare and unique items, and discrete collections that represent key eras of quilting scholarship or are based on extensive ethnographic and archival research. The MSU Museum now holds more than 500 significant historical and contemporary quilts. The quilt collections are housed in state-of-the-art rolled storage system in the museum's Cultural Collections Resource Center.

The New England Quilt Museum:

It was almost 30 years ago that a group of enthusiastic New England quilters began to dream of establishing a regional quilt museum. That dream became a reality when the New England Quilt Museum in historic Lowell, Massachusetts first opened its doors in in 1987. Now, as its 25th anniversary year has come and gone (in 2012), it seems miraculous that the museum exists and has survived and grown, fulfilling the mission first conceived by its founding mothers. The permanent collection includes some 400 antique and contemporary quilts and tops, plus numerous related textile and sewing items that represent the history of American quilting.